FROM THE PROTESTANT REFORMATION TO THE SOUTHERN BAPTIST CONVENTION

WHAT HATH GENEVA TO DO WITH NASHVILLE?

FROM THE PROTESTANT REFORMATION TO THE SOUTHERN BAPTIST CONVENTION

WHAT HATH GENEVA TO DO WITH NASHVILLE?

REVISED EDITION
INCLUDING THE CHARLESTON
CONFESSION OF FAITH
AND A SUMMARY OF CHURCH DISCIPLINE

THOMAS K. ASCOL

 Founders Press

Committed to historic Baptist principles
Cape Coral, Florida

Published by

Founders Press

Committed to historic Baptist principles
Cape Coral, Florida

P.O. Box 150931 • Cape Coral, FL 33915
Phone (239) 772–1400 • Fax: (239) 772–1140
Electronic Mail: founders@founders.org
Website: http://www.founders.org

Revised Edition ©2013 Founders Press
First Edition ©1996 Founders Press
Printed in the United States of America

ISBN 13: 978–0–9785711–6–0

Cover photo: Mont Blanc

CONTENTS

FOREWORD

Baptists have often been classified, and sometimes shunned, as separatists. Indeed, in a number of cases they felt conscience-bound to separate themselves from others whose faith and/or life were judged to be so much at variance from what they believed the Bible to teach, that a continued ecclesial unity would be irresponsible. On the other hand, they often found opportunity to unite with other Christians in spite of differences in their origin and some distinct nuances in their creedal formulations.

In this book, Tom Ascol profitably points to the union of three original groups of Baptists in the South who united in order to form the Southern Baptist Convention in 1845. And their convictions were "Reformed" or "Calvinist," as some call them, although Calvin was not the author of such views, but only one theologian who clearly saw them taught in Scripture and expounded them with peculiar power and skill.

Roger Nicole (1915–2010)
Founding member and past president
of the Evangelical Theological Society

INTRODUCTION

In 1996 Founders Press was launched with the modest offering of a small booklet entitled, *From the Protestant Reformation to the Southern Baptist Convention: What Hath Geneva to Do with Nashville?* The purpose of the booklet was to help argue the historical point that Southern Baptists have much in common with other Protestant heirs of the Reformation. Specifically, the concern was to demonstrate that the doctrinal heritage of the SBC is firmly entrenched in that Reformed theology known as the "doctrines of grace."

To most Baptists who have taken the time to investigate our denominational roots, that point seems hardly debatable today. Even the most strident opponents of the sovereignty of God's grace in salvation (well, for the most part) now recognize that dimensions of Reformed theology influenced the origins of the SBC. Sometimes that influence is minimized to one of two or more "streams" that conflated to form the convention, but at least it is acknowledged.

The issue of Southern Baptist origins is not really of supreme importance. Far more significant than what was once believed is what the Bible actually says. But history does have some important lessons to teach us. Humility dictates that we consider the theological convictions of those on whose shoulders we stand. We owe them this consideration because of their many labors that still benefit us today. We owe it to ourselves because if what they believed was true in their day, then it is still true in our day because God's truth does not change.

From the Protestant Reformation uses a historical argument in order to make that theological point. What our forefathers believed and taught about the nature of God's saving grace is worthy of our careful study. They were men committed to the authority and clarity of God's Word just as strongly as we are today. They did exegesis and exposition just as we do. We should be willing to listen to them.

Perhaps they were wrong. If we become convinced of that then let's be bold to state it plainly. If we are unwilling to make that conclusion, then let's allow for the legitimacy of their doctrinal views and not fight against the growing recovery of them in our day. Baptists have a rich theological heritage. Lessons from that heritage can serve us well as we chart a God-glorifying course for the future.

FROM THE PROTESTANT REFORMATION TO THE SOUTHERN BAPTIST CONVENTION

WHAT HATH GENEVA TO DO WITH NASHVILLE?

Sometimes Baptists live under the mistaken notion that they came into existence with little or no influence from any other evangelical group. Some even believe that Baptist churches have existed from the time of John "the Baptist" to the present. While the principles that Baptists hold dear originate in the Word of God and have been found in various degrees of purity throughout church history, our origin as a distinct group can be traced to the early seventeenth century.

Modern Baptists arose out of the spiritual impetus of the sixteenth-century Protestant Reformation. We are a Reformational people. In many respects the seat of the Reformation in Europe was Geneva where John Calvin helped train countless pastors, missionaries and future martyrs to preach the gospel throughout the world. The Scottish Reformer, John Knox, called the academy established there "the most perfect school of Christ that ever was on earth since the days of the Apostles."[1]

---

[1] Hans J. Hillerbrand, ed., *The Reformation, a Narrative History Related by Contemporary Observers and Participants* (Grand Rapids, MI: Baker Book House, 1981), 173.

The Southern Baptist Convention came into existence in 1845. Over the years Nashville, Tennessee has become home to the offices of the SBC Executive Committee as well as the Sunday School Board (now called LifeWay). Although local churches hold the final authority in our denominational polity, Nashville has become symbolic as the "headquarters" of what has become the largest missionary sending agency in the world.

As disjointed as the worlds of sixteenth-century Geneva and twenty-first–century Nashville may appear, there is in reality a close and vital connection between them. The relationship becomes apparent when we trace some of the main features of the Southern Baptist family tree.

We Baptists look to the Scriptures to justify our existence, and that is just as it should be. We are a people of the Book. The Bible, and the Bible alone, is our authority. We look no further than the Scriptures to seek direction for our faith and practice. History is not our authority. Nevertheless, history can be our assistant as we learn from the biblical insights of those who have gone before us. In this day when it seems that an identity crisis is epidemic among Baptists, especially among those known as Southern Baptists, wisdom dictates that we consider afresh our heritage and take note of how the Lord taught and guided our forefathers who were committed to the Baptist way in the face of great challenges and struggles.

The heritage of Southern Baptists is rich, and it stretches back hundreds of years before our actual formation as a denomination in 1845. Our roots extend all the way back to the fertile soil of the sixteenth-century Protestant Reformation.

The revised edition of this small work includes two very valuable appendices. The first is a reprint of the *Charleston Confession of Faith*, adopted by the Charleston Baptist Association in 1767

(Appendix A). The association adopted *A Summary of Church Discipline* in 1773 (Appendix B) and the next year published it together with the Confession. These two influential documents from the rich Baptist heritage in America are of lasting value not only historically but also for their serious engagement of the biblical text both theologically and practically.

From the Protestant Reformation to 1619

The nineteenth-century Scottish theologian William Cunningham called the Protestant Reformation "the greatest event, or series of events, that has occurred since the close of the canon of Scripture."[2] It was, quite simply, a great work of the Spirit of God, a revival of biblical Christianity. Without a doubt, the Reformation stands as the most significant revival since Apostolic times.

General Characteristics of the Reformation

Before an obscure monk named Martin Luther nailed ninety-five theses to the church door at Wittenburg on October 31, 1517, the church of Christ had been living in spiritually dark times. The Bible had been kept from the common people. The Roman Catholic Church had largely perverted the gospel of God's grace by teaching that salvation comes from the hands

---

[2] William Cunningham, *The Reformers and the Theology of the Reformation* (first published 1862; reprint edition, Edinburgh: The Banner of Truth Trust, 1989), 1.

of the priests through the administration of the sacraments in response to human works and merit.

With the dawning of the Reformation these perversions of the gospel were exposed, and a renewal of biblical Christianity emerged. The story of how this awakening emerged and spread across Europe and Great Britain is a fascinating one and demonstrates the kindness of God's providence.[3] What follows is only an overview of what happened and, more specifically, what resulted from the Reformation.

With the rediscovery of the Bible in the sixteenth century came a reawakening to God's way of salvation by grace alone through faith alone in Christ alone. In fact, that little word alone provides a real key to understanding the main themes of the Reformation. In Latin the word is sola and it was used in five phrases that capture the essence of Reformational theology.

Five Reformation Themes

1. SOLA SCRIPTURA: SCRIPTURE ALONE

The Reformers taught that the Scripture alone is the final authority for what we must believe and how we must live. This view sounds commonplace to us today, but it was radical in the sixteenth century. For centuries the Roman Catholic Church

---

[3] Among the many excellent treatments of this era are Kenneth Scott Latourette, *A History of Christianity*, Volume 2: A.D. 1500–1975, revised edition (San Francisco, CA: Harper Collins, 1997), 689–835 and Hans J. Hillerbrand, editor, *The Reformation: A Narrative History Related by Contemporary Observers and Participants* (Grand Rapids, MI: Baker Book House, 1978).

had asserted its authority over against that of the Bible. The authority of the Pope, tradition and councils were all regarded as determinative along with the Bible. Against that view, the Reformers asserted *sola Scriptura*: the Bible, and the Bible alone, is our only infallible source of authority for faith and practice.

2. Sola Gratia: Grace Alone

How can a sinful man become right with a holy God? That is always the most important religious question. It was the question that plagued Luther's conscience and nearly drove him insane before he was converted. Rome had developed a very elaborate system in response to that question. Rome's answer involved human works and merit—a sinner must perform sufficiently well before God if he would receive the blessing of salvation.

But through the study of the Scriptures the Reformers rediscovered that salvation is the gracious gift of God. Man contributes nothing to it. It is only by the sheer, absolute grace of God. Bible words like *election* and *predestination*, which magnify the grace of God in salvation, were rediscovered, having been largely forgotten or drained of their meaning by the mainstream of medieval Roman Catholic teachers.[4]

---

[4] There were, of course, notable exceptions. A small but stubborn stream of teachers who insisted on predestination and election can be traced throughout the middle ages. Among them were Gottschalk of Orbais, Thomas Bradwardine and Gregory of Rimini.

3. Sola Fide: Faith Alone

The Reformers taught that the means whereby a sinner is graciously justified before God is faith—not faith plus merit or faith plus works—but faith alone. Luther discovered that the Bible teaches that the sinner must place his trust in Jesus Christ in order to gain a right standing before God. Through faith alone the righteousness of Jesus Christ is imputed to the one who believes thereby rendering him justified before God.

4. Solus Christus: Christ Alone

The Reformation rejected Rome's requirement that common church members put their faith implicitly in the church's teachings. Instead, they argued, Jesus Christ alone is the proper object of faith. He is to be trusted for salvation—not priests, popes, councils or traditions. To require anything more than Christ is in effect to detract from Christ since He and He alone is the sufficient Savior for all who trust Him.

5. Soli Deo Gloria: The Glory of God Alone

In one sense the Reformation can be seen as a rediscovery of God—a reawakening to the greatness and grandeur of the God of the Bible. It is God, not man, who belongs at the center of our thoughts and view of the world. And it is God's glory alone that is to occupy first place in our motivations and desires as His children. He created the world and us for Himself, and He redeemed us for Himself. Our purpose is to glorify Him.

Certainly there are other truths that would need to be discussed in a thorough consideration of Reformation theology, but these themes summarize the essence of Reformed thought. It is obvious that the Reformers did not invent these teachings. They simply rediscovered them in the Bible and brought them out into the light for all of God's people to experience. Baptists have been greatly influenced by these Reformed themes.

John Calvin

The most systematic exponent of Reformation theology was John Calvin, the Reformer of Geneva. His *Institutes of the Christian Religion* is a classic whose value is recognized by his followers and critics alike. Sadly, Calvin is more often vilified than read in our day. It has become quite fashionable among some Baptists to caricature his ministry and his teaching. He is often ignorantly portrayed as a harsh, prideful, sinister heretic-burner. For example, Joe Underwood, writing for *Baptists Today*, has erroneously charged that Calvin "ordered (and secured) the bloody, or fiery, execution of hundreds who disagreed with his doctrine and discipline."[5]

It is true that one man, the Unitarian Michael Servetus, was executed in Geneva in 1553 because of his anti-Trinitarian views. That was a tragic event—one of many such tragedies that occurred well into the seventeenth century throughout Europe and England where church and state were joined together. While we can never justify the burning of heretics in the sixteenth century, neither can we overlook the harsh realities of that cultural context. Calvin was a man of his times.

[5] Joe Underwood, "Retired Missions Leader Wonders if Loyalty is to Calvin or Jesus?" *Baptists Today* (March 9, 1995), 16.

But Calvin was also one of the most gifted expositors and systematizers of God's Word that the world has ever seen. From the Scriptures he argued that God is sovereign over every aspect of life—including man's salvation. Everything and everyone has come from God, was created for God, and will ultimately bring glory to God. Calvin clearly grasped and simply taught the depravity of the human race, which has left men without spiritual ability to come to Christ by their own power. He emphasized the glory of God in the grace of Jesus Christ that works to save sinners. Calvin expounded the biblical themes of election and predestination, showing them to be the unconditional blessings of God's sheer grace, which guarantee the salvation of helpless, lost sinners. He explained that the death of Jesus provided a definite atonement for sin, and that because of that death, sinners can be forgiven of sin and reconciled to God. Such reconciliation is effected, Calvin said, through the powerful work of the Holy Spirit when He effectually calls sinners to Christ through the proclamation of the gospel.

All of this is what is typically meant when someone speaks of "Calvinism" or "Reformed theology." Neither term is usually employed as a reference to everything that Calvin or the other Reformers taught. Calvin's views on infant baptism, church-state relationship, church officers, and government are rejected outright by many who would nevertheless describe themselves as Calvinists (including the author). "Calvinism" is a worldview. It sees creation, history and salvation from a God-centered perspective. In particular, "Calvinism" is used primarily as a soteriological term. It is a short-hand reference to those biblical doctrines that magnify the glory and grace of God in salvation.

Charles Spurgeon speaks for his fellow proponents of "Calvinism" when he says, "I love to proclaim these strong old doctrines, which are called by nickname Calvinism, but which are surely and verily the revealed truth of God as it is in Christ Jesus."[6]

Synod of Dort, 1618–19

This view, which sees God at the center of salvation, stands in stark contrast to the more man-centered view of Arminianism, modified dimensions of which have become prevalent in our day. The difference between these two positions was made plain by the deliberations that took place at the Synod of Dort in 1618 and 1619.

Arminianism

When Calvin died in 1564, Jacob Arminius was four years old. He grew up to become a student of Theodore Beza, who was Calvin's successor at Geneva. In the course of preparing a defense of his teacher's view of predestination, Arminius became convinced of the opposing position. He went on to reject unconditional election and predestination and taught instead that God elects people based on His foreknowledge that they will exercise faith in Christ.

By the time he died in 1609, Arminius' views had been widely promulgated and debated throughout the Netherlands. The debate intensified the year after his death when his followers, called the Remonstrants, drew up five statements set-

---

[6] "Election," a sermon preached September 2, 1855. See Spurgeon, *The New Park Street Pulpit*, Volume 1, reprint edition (Pasadena, TX: Pilgrim Publications, 1981), 313.

ting forth the views of Arminianism. Arminian theology was in essence a rationalizing of Calvinism. It attempted to remove the tension between God's sovereignty and man's responsibility by diminishing the significance of the former. The synod of the Dutch Reformed Church convened at the city of Dort in 1618 and 1619 to deal with the Remonstrant articles.

The five points of the Arminians may be summarized as follows:

1. God elects or does not elect on the basis of foreseen faith or unbelief.

2. Christ died for every man, although only believers are saved.

3. Man is not so corrupted by sin that he cannot savingly believe the gospel when it is put before him.[7]

4. God's saving grace may be resisted.

5. Those who are in Christ may or may not fall finally away.

CALVINISM

After seven months and 154 sessions the synod rejected the Remonstrant articles (the five points of Arminianism) and published their view of the doctrines that had been called into question. These Canons of Dort consist of fifty-nine articles with thirty-four additional paragraphs. They were published under

---

[7] J. I. Packer, "Introductory Essay" in John Owens, *The Death of Death in the Death of Christ* (Edinburgh: The Banner of Truth Trust, 1959), 3.

five "heads of doctrine" (with the third and fourth being printed together) and have come to be known as the "five points" of Calvinism.

The so-called five points of Calvinism as they were expressed at Dort may be summarized as follows:

1. Election is the unchangeable purpose of God whereby, before the foundation of the world, He, out of mere grace and according to His sovereign good pleasure, chose certain persons to be redeemed by Christ.

2. The death of Christ is "of infinite worth and value, abundantly sufficient to expiate the sins of the whole world" (Article III). The saving efficacy of that death extends only to the elect because "it was the will of God that Christ by the blood of the cross, whereby he confirmed the new covenant, should effectually redeem out of every people, tribe, nation and language all those, and those only, who were from eternity chosen to salvation and given to him by the Father" (Article VIII).

3. Though man was originally created upright, because of the Fall, "all men are conceived in sin, by nature children of wrath, incapable of any saving good, prone to evil, dead in sin, and in bondage thereto; and, without the regenerating grace of the Holy Spirit, they are neither able nor willing to return to God" (Article III).

4. Those whom God chose from eternity in Christ, He calls effectually in time and "confers upon them faith and repentance, rescues them from the power of darkness, and translates them into the kingdom of his own dear Son" (Article X). God does this by causing the gospel to be externally preached to them and powerfully illuminating

their minds by His Holy Spirit, so that they may rightly understand and discern the things of the Spirit of God. By the Spirit's work of regeneration He pervades the inmost recesses of a man; He opens the closed heart and softens the hardened heart and infuses new qualities into the will, which, though heretofore dead, He quickens (Article XI).

5. Those whom God effectually calls do not totally fall from faith and grace. Though they may temporarily fall into backslidings, they will persevere to the end and be saved.

The order of these "contra-remonstrant" articles has been re-arranged to facilitate the use of an acrostic as an aid to memory: T-U-L-I-P—Total Depravity, Unconditional Election, Limited Atonement, Irresistible Grace and Perseverance of the Saints. This is what is meant by the five points of Calvinism, or, as they are sometimes called, "the doctrines of grace." Once again, it is not accurate simply to reduce Calvinism to these five points. Rather, Calvinsm is a way of viewing the world that stems from a clear vision of the sovereignty of God in creation, providence and salvation. These five points do clarify the Calvinistic under-standing of the gospel, but they in no way say everything that Calvinism declares about salvation.

HYPER-CALVINISM

It might be beneficial to distinguish Calvinism from hyper-Calvinism because the two are often confused.[8] Indeed, some

[8] One of the finest treatments of true Calvinism and hyper-Calvinism is Iain Murray, *Spurgeon v. Hyper-Calvinism: The Battle for Gospel Preaching* (Edinburgh: The Banner of Truth Trust, 1995).

writers and teachers confuse them so often and so willingly that one must wonder if the practice is intentional. In one sense, hyper-Calvinism, like Arminianism, is a rationalistic perversion of true Calvinism. Whereas Arminianism destroys the sovereignty of God, hyper-Calvinism destroys the responsibility of man. The irony is that both Arminianism and hyper-Calvinism start from the same, erroneous rationalistic presupposition: *Man's ability and responsibility are coextensive.* That is, they must match up exactly or else it is irrational. If a man is to be held responsible for something, then he must have the ability to do it. On the other hand, if a man does not have the ability to perform it, he cannot be obligated to do it.

The Arminian looks at this premise and says, "Agreed! We know that all men are held responsible to repent and believe the gospel [which is true, according to the Bible]; therefore we must conclude that all men have the ability in themselves to repent and believe [which is false, according to the Bible]." Thus, Arminians teach that unconverted people have within themselves the spiritual ability to repent and believe.

The hyper-Calvinist takes the same premise (that man's ability and responsibility are coextensive) and says, "Agreed! We know that, in and of themselves, all men are without spiritual ability to repent and believe [which is true, according to the Bible]; therefore we must conclude that unconverted people are not under obligation to repent and believe the gospel [which is false, according to the Bible]."

In contrast to both of these, the Calvinist looks at the premise and says, "Wrong! While it looks reasonable, it is not biblical. The Bible teaches both that fallen man is without spiritual ability *and* that he is obligated to repent and believe. Only by the powerful, regenerating work of the Holy Spirit is man given the ability to fulfill his duty to repent and believe." And though that may be judged unreasonable to rationalistic minds, it merely appears to be so. There is no contradiction between the complete responsibility of man and the absolute sovereignty of God. They are both true at the same time. This is precisely the position the Bible teaches.

It is completely untenable, therefore, to accuse true Calvinism of being rationalistic, as is sometimes done today. While it certainly is reasonable, unlike both Arminianism and hyper-Calvinism, it refuses to superimpose on the Scripture philosophical conclusions from rationalistic presuppositions. Calvinism starts with Scripture and ends with Scripture, believing whatever has been revealed and seeking to understand and affirm that revelation, regardless what canons of rationalism are violated in the process.[9]

Why are these things so important to our discussion? Because Baptists have been confronted with these theological issues throughout their history. The Arminianism–Calvinism–Hyper-Calvinism debate has played a decisive role in shaping our identity as Baptists, and particularly our identity as Southern Baptists.

[9] The difference between being rational and being a rationalist should be kept clear. The former is simply following the rules of logic and is seen repeatedly in Scripture. See, for example, the letters of Paul and his explanation of his testimony before Agrippa and Festus as recorded in Acts 26:25, "I am not mad, most noble Festus, but speak the words of truth and reason."

The Emergence of Modern Baptists in England

While the Calvinism-Arminianism debate was raging in Holland in the early seventeenth century, other forces were at work in England that ultimately resulted in the rise of modern Baptists.

In the last half of the sixteenth century the Puritan movement began to emerge in England. Although they did not all share the same ecclesiastical goal, Puritans, Separatists and Independents were all essentially English Calvinists. It is from this common source (perhaps with some influence from Continental Anabaptists) that the two streams of Baptists in England originated. One was Arminian and the other was Calvinistic.

General Baptists

The Baptist denomination began in the seventeenth century in England. A man named John Smyth, who had been brought up in the Calvinist-Puritan tradition, came to question a number of the ideas that he had been taught, especially infant baptism. After being exiled with his congregation to Holland, Smyth became convinced that he needed to be baptized as a believer. In January of 1609 Smyth poured water over himself and Thomas Helwys as an expression of believers' baptism. They then baptized the remainder of the congregation.

Smyth and his followers were strongly influenced by the Arminian view of salvation. They were called "General Baptists" because they held to a universal or general view of the atonement (i.e., that Jesus died for no one in particular but for everyone in general). Smyth did not remain a Baptist long. He soon joined the Mennonites. Helwys led the church back to England in 1611, where he was imprisoned for his views on religious liberty. This group represents the first modern Baptist church on English soil.

The Arminian Baptists were unable to spread their principles very far. By 1626 there were only six General Baptist churches in England with a total membership of around 100. These churches eventually drifted from Arminianism into Unitarianism and actually died out in the next century. A "new connection" of General Baptist churches was organized in 1770 and, under the leadership of Dan Taylor, continued on into the nineteenth century.

Particular Baptists

The other group of Baptists to emerge in seventeenth century England went by the name of "Particular Baptists." Like their Arminian counterparts, their name reflects their theology, being a reference to their Calvinistic view of Christ's atonement as definite, or particular. That is, they believed that Jesus' death did not merely make salvation *possible* for everyone in general. Rather, they understood the Bible to teach that Jesus actually *paid* for the sins of His particular people—His elect—when He died on the cross. These Particular or Calvinistic Baptists emerged during the 1630s when a Calvinistic Separatist church came to believe that baptism should be administered only to believers.

The Particular Baptists went on to affirm not only believers' baptism but believers' baptism by *immersion*. By 1641, at the latest, there existed a Baptist church that practiced baptism by immersion.

The Particular Baptists began to suffer under false accusations from their theological opponents. They were accused of being Pelagian in their view of sin and man, of being Anabaptists, of being General Baptists and of being anarchists. In order to declare openly their principles (with a special concern to distance themselves from the Anabaptists and General Baptists), the seven Particular Baptist churches of London decided to publish a confession of faith in 1644. As William Lumpkin has argued, "Perhaps no Confession of Faith has had so formative an influence on Baptist life as this one."[10] It clarified the distinctive, Baptist view of the church while affirming the Reformed view of salvation.

This *First London Confession* served Baptists well until the latter part of the century, when Baptists, Presbyterians and Congregationalists began to suffer persecution under the harsh restrictions of the Clarendon Code adopted by Parliament. In an effort to show their substantial doctrinal unity with their fellow sufferers who were paedobaptistic, the Particular Baptists called for an assembly, which met in London in 1677 to draw up another confession of faith. It was modeled primarily on the *Westminster Confession* of the Presbyterians and, to a lesser degree, on the *Savoy Declaration* of the Congregationalists.

The framers of this *Second London Confession* did not regard themselves as moving away from that which had been affirmed in the 1644 Confession. In fact, they observed that the *Westminster* (1646) and *Savoy* (1658) actually followed the same theological convictions as the earlier Baptist Confession—not at every point, obviously, but certainly on the main issues. The Preface of the *Second London Confession* makes this obvious in its

---

[10] William L. Lumpkin, *Baptist Confessions of Faith*, revised edition (Valley Forge, PA: Judson Press, 1969), 152.

explanation of why the framers believed a new confession was necessary:

> "Forasmuch as that Confession is not now commonly to be had; and also that many others have since embraced the same truth which is owned therein; it was judged necessary by us to joyn [sic] together in giving a testimony to the world; of our firm adhering to those wholesome Principles, by the publication of this which is now in your hand."[11]

Because of the political climate, this *Second London Confession* was not published openly until 1689 when it was issued with the endorsement of 107 Baptist churches across England and Wales.

While the General Baptists were degenerating into Unitarianism in the eighteenth century, the Particular Baptists began to decline through the parasitic influence of hyper-Calvinism. Although they remained orthodox in belief, many—but not all—Particular Baptist churches became hardened by a fatalistic spirit. One hymn from this period[12] exemplifies their attitude:

> We are the Lord's elected few,
> Let all the rest be damned.
> There's room enough in hell for you,
> We'll not have heaven crammed!

[11] Ibid., 244.

[12] Timothy George, *Theology of the Reformers* (Nashville, TN: Broadman Press, 1988), 233.

Fortunately, this hyper-Calvinism did not go unchecked. Ultimately it was challenged and overcome in the late eighteenth century by Andrew Fuller, William Carey, John Suttcliffe and others. These men and their colleagues rejected what they called "false Calvinism" and returned to the evangelical Calvinism (what they called "true or strict Calvinism") of their Particular Baptist forefathers. This revitalized Reformed theology gave birth to the modern missionary movement with the formation of the Particular Baptist Missionary Society in 1792. It was with the assistance of this society that William Carey—the "father of the modern missionary movement"—made his way to India.

Baptists in America

In the seventeenth century both General and Particular Baptists joined others in the quest for religious freedom by sailing to America. The Particular Baptists were the first actually to organize churches in the new land. Though he remained a Baptist for only a short while, Roger Williams founded the first Baptist church in America in Providence, Rhode Island, in 1639. The next year John Clarke established a Baptist church in Newport, Rhode Island, which by 1644 had adopted immersion as the proper mode of baptism.

Overall, General Baptists fared far better than their Calvinistic counterparts in the New England colonies. In the Middle Colonies and the South, however, it was the Particular Baptists who took the lead. The development and character of Baptist work in the South is reflected in the organization and outreach of early associations. The first three Baptist associations in America were also the three most influential in shaping the faith and practice of Baptist churches in the South.

The Philadelphia Association

Pennsylvania proved to be fertile soil for Baptist work in the eighteenth century. The first Baptist church was formed there in Pennepek in 1688 by Elias Keach, the son of the famous Benjamin Keach, a Particular Baptist pastor in England. Through the younger Keach's strenuous labors several other churches were planted in and around Philadelphia. In 1707 five of these churches joined to form the Philadelphia Association, which not only was the first but also soon became the most influential Baptist Association in America. These congregations recognized the *1689 Second London Confession* as their own. In 1742 they formally adopted a version of that confession which Benjamin and Elias Keach had slightly edited to include articles on hymn singing and laying on of hands. It is known as the *Philadelphia Baptist Confession.*

These churches were so crystal clear in their affirmation of Calvinism that one former Southern Baptist theologian derisively referred to the association as the "Philadelphia Synod" and to the church members as "baptizing Presbyterians."[13] The Philadelphia Association sent numerous missionaries and church planters throughout the South during the middle and latter eighteenth century. It was responsible for the rapid growth of "Regular Baptist" (which is what Calvinistic Baptists came to be called) churches and associations in the South.

[13] Molly Marshall, at the inaugural Hoover Lectures at Richmond Seminary, April, 1995; tape transcript.

Timothy George has noted that the Philadelphia Confession "became the most widely accepted, definitive confession among Baptists in America both North and South. Each of the 293 'delegates,' as they were then called, who gathered in Augusta to organize the Southern Baptist Convention in 1845, belonged to congregations and associations which had adopted the Philadelphia/Charleston Confession of Faith as their own."[14]

The Charleston Association

The next influential association in the South was the Charleston Baptist Association. It also has the distinction of being the first association on southern soil. The First Baptist Church of Charleston was instrumental in organizing the association. This church, which was the first Baptist church in the South, was actually founded in Kittery, Maine, in 1682 by William Screven. It began as a Particular Baptist church, having formally adopted the *Second London Confession*. In 1696 Screven

---

[14] Timothy and Denise George, general editors, *Baptist Confessions, Covenants, and Catechisms* (Nashville, TN: Broadman and Holman, 1996), 11. George goes on to note the prominent influence which this confession had on early Southern Baptist theological education: "When James P. Boyce was considering a suitable confessional standard for Southern Baptists' first seminary, he originally planned to use the Philadelphia/Charleston Confession of Faith as the doctrinal basis for this new institution. When he became convinced that a brief, succinct summary of doctrine would be more useful for this purpose, he commissioned Basil Manly, Jr., to draft an Abstract of Principles based on the Philadelphia/Charleston standard" (Ibid).

and the congregation moved to Charleston, where four years later they reaffirmed their adherence to the *1689 Confession*.[15]

In 1751, under the leadership of Oliver Hart and the influence of the Philadelphia Association, the Charleston Association was founded. Sixteen years later, in 1767, the association adopted the *Second London Confession* (see Appendix A). Through the influence and missionary efforts of this association across the South, Reformation theology became even more firmly embedded in the Baptist movement.

The Sandy Creek Association (Separate Baptist)

The Great Awakening that swept through the American colonies in the 1730s and 1740s made a significant impact on Baptists in two ways. First, the comparatively few Baptist churches that existed at the time were directly affected by the revival and saw tremendous growth in their memberships. Second, many Congregationalist churches that developed out of the revival eventually became Baptist. One historian has described these "New Light" Congregational churches as "halfway house[s] on the road to becoming Baptists."[16] Most of these who made the change to believers' baptism had been converted under George

---

[15] *The Charleston Confession of Faith, A Summary of Church Discipline*, and *The Baptist Catechism*, all of which were published by the Charleston Association, have been recently reprinted under the title, *Some Southern Documents* (Birmingham, AL: Society for Biblical and Southern Studies, 1995).

[16] W.G. McLoughlin, quoted in H. Leon McBeth, *The Baptist Heritage: Four Centuries of Baptist Witness* (Nashville, TN: Broadman Press, 1987), 205.

Whitefield. This phenomenon caused the great evangelist to muse, "My chickens are becoming ducks!"[17] Baptists gained over a hundred new churches this way in addition to gaining some of their most outstanding leaders, such as Isaac Backus, Daniel Marshall and Shubal Stearns.[18]

These churches born out of revival became known as "Separate Baptist," and they saw rapid growth in the South and on the frontier. The most incredible display of such growth came through the ministry of Shubal Stearns and his brother-in-law, Daniel Marshall.

In 1755 Stearns and Marshall moved to Sandy Creek, North Carolina, where they started the first Separate Baptist church in the South. They began with sixteen people and within three years had three fully constituted churches with a combined membership of over 900. In only seventeen years this church gave birth to forty-two churches and sent out 125 ministers.

In 1758 the Sandy Creek Association was formed. The Separate Baptist churches that joined together in forming it had a healthy skepticism regarding confessions and creeds. Their skepticism grew out of experience with the dead orthodoxy they had left behind in Congregationalism. This position distinguished

[17] Robert Baker, normally a careful historian, reported, "No wonder George Whitefield, a Church of England Methodist who disdained the use of much water in baptizing infants or adults, as he pondered how he had helped produce many Baptists who immersed their candidates fully into the baptismal pool, ruefully said, 'All my chickens have become ducks.'" [Robert A. Baker, *The Southern Baptist Convention and its People*, (Nashville, TN: Broadman Press, 1974), 48. Others have attributed this comment to William Grimshaw.

[18] McBeth, *The Baptist Heritage*, 203.

them from the Regular Baptists, who were enthusiastically confessional in their churches. However, this distinction must not be stretched beyond what the historical record will bear.

Regular Baptists, Separate Baptists and Calvinism

Some historians have interpreted the Separate Baptist "aversion to creeds" to mean that they were opposed to doctrinal precision in general and to Reformed theology in particular. The "Sandy Creek tradition," as it has been called, has been unjustly described as consisting of an evangelistic zeal that was in some sense hostile to the Calvinism of the Regular Baptists. According to this perspective it "minimized Calvinism and emphasized evangelism."[19] Similarly, the "Charleston tradition" has often

---

[19] Fisher Humphreys, *The Way We Were: How Southern Baptist Theology Has Changed and What it Means to Us All* (New York: McCracken Press, 1994), 85. Humphreys follows the view of Walter Shurden as set forth in "The 1980–81 Carver-Barnes Lectures" (Wake Forest, NC: Southeastern Baptist Theological Seminary, 1980). William G. McLoughlin sees the distinctions between Separate and Regular Baptists as having little or nothing to do with Calvinism. Both groups were, in his estimation, convinced of Calvinistic theology. When describing the decline of the General, or Arminian Baptists of New England in the late eighteenth century, McLoughlin parenthetically identifies the Baptists who were "Calvinists" as "the Separate Baptists." He further explains that "in the South the Calvinists split into two wings, the Regular, or Particular Baptists (led by evangelists from the Philadelphia Baptist Association like [Benjamin] Miller and [Peter P.] Van Horne), and the Separates (led by New England Separate Baptists)" in *The Diary of Isaac Backus* (Providence, RI: Brown University Press, 1979), 3:1246.

been mischaracterized as being Calvinistic but not evangelistic. The historical record, however, simply will not bear this judgment. The following three reasons are sufficient to make this plain.

1. Regular Baptists were thoroughly evangelistic

In the first place, the Calvinism of the Regular Baptists was thoroughly evangelical, as the work of the Philadelphia and Charleston Associations clearly demonstrate.[20] The parasite of hyper-Calvinism did develop in some churches (especially in Kentucky), but this was rightly regarded as a perversion of Reformed theology.[21] Evangelistic concern, therefore, would not have been foreign to Regular Baptists, nor would Separate Baptists have thought it to be so. The eventual union of Regular and Separate Baptists in the South was not at all encumbered by any perceived lack of evangelistic concern on the part of the Regulars.

During Oliver Hart's ministry as pastor of the First Baptist Church of Charleston, the congregation sent a request to the meeting of the Charleston Association in November, 1755. They asked the association to secure a missionary to labor among the destitute people "in the interior settlements of this and neigh-

[20] See McBeth, *The Baptist Heritage*, 239–42.
[21] See George W. Purefoy, *A History of the Sandy Creek Baptist Association* (first published New York: Sheldon & Co., 1859; reprint edition, New York: Arno Press, 1980), 55–60, in which Purefoy calls the hyper-Calvinists, "The New Baptists."

boring States."[22] This took place *before* Daniel Marshall and Shubal Stearns migrated from Opekon, Virginia to begin the Separate Baptist movement at Sandy Creek. In response to the church's request, the association commissioned John Gano to preach the gospel at the Jersey Settlement on the banks of the Yadkin River—not far from Sandy Creek—in what is now North Carolina. Far from being a dividing point, Sandy Creek actually became something of a meeting point for the evangelistic fervor of both the Charleston and Separate Baptists.

Furthermore, a later pastor of FBC Charleston, Richard Furman, helped organize the General Missionary Convention (Triennial Convention) in 1814. At the organizational meeting on May 21 of that year, the delegates asked Furman to preach. His closing appeal clearly refutes the charge that "Charleston Calvinists" were something less than concerned for evangelism and missions.

> Let the wise and good employ their counsels; the minister of Christ, who is qualified for the sacred service, offer himself for the work; the man of wealth and generosity, who values the glory of Immanuel and the salvation of souls more than gold, bring of his treasure in proportion as God has bestowed on him; yea, let all, even the pious widow, bring the mite that can be spared; and let all who fear and love God, unite in the prayer of faith before the throne of Grace; and unceasingly say, "Thy Kingdom come." And O! let it never be forgotten, that the Son of God hath said: "Lo, I am with you always, even to the end of the world." Amen and Amen.[23]

---

[22] Cited in Robert A. Baker and Paul J. Craven, Jr., *Adventure in Faith, the First 300 Years of First Baptist Church, Charleston, South Carolina* (Nashville, TN: Broadman Press, 1982), 156.

[23] Ibid., 196.

By 1845, the year of the founding of the SBC, the Triennial convention had compiled an impressive missions record: they had missionaries among eight Indian groups in North America; in numerous European countries as well as in Africa, Burma, Siam, China, Assam, India and other parts of Asia. "The total program by 1845 involved 17 missions; 130 mission stations and outstations; 109 missionaries and assistant missionaries, of whom 42 were preachers; 123 native preachers and assistants; 79 churches, 2,593 baptisms in the previous year, and more than 5,000 church members; and 1,350 students in 56 schools."[24]

Furman also led his church to participate in a "Quarterly Concert of Prayer for world missions" and recommended this practice to all the churches of the association by 1795. After 1810, the church held this prayer meeting on the first Monday of every month.[25]

In 1800 the General Committee of the Charleston Association called on that body to engage even more diligently in the concerted work of missions.

> Is there not at this time, a call in providence for our churches to make the most serious exertions, in union with other Christians of various denominations, to send the gospel among the heathen; or to such people who, though living in countries where the gospel revelation is known, do not enjoy a standing ministry, and the regular administration of divine ordinances among them?[26]

[24] Ibid., 232.
[25] Ibid., 221–22.
[26] Ibid., 226.

It is obvious from these examples that the Regular Baptists were energetically engaged in the work of evangelism and missions.

2. Separate Baptists came from a Reformed background and were very Calvinistic

Secondly, it must not be forgotten that the Separate Baptists came from a background of Congregationalism, which had as its confessional foundation the *Savoy Declaration*—a thoroughly Reformed confession of faith. Those who separated from Congregationalism after the Great Awakening did so not because they rejected Reformed theology but because they rejected a dead formalism that substituted agreement with a creed for vital, experiential Christianity. Separate Baptists were not without theological convictions. The insights we have into their convictions indicate an agreement with that Calvinistic understanding of salvation that has been handed down from the Protestant Reformation.[27]

[27] This point is clearly demonstrated by comparing the two confessions of faith which Isaac Backus wrote for churches he served. Before coming to Baptist convictions, Backus wrote a confession and covenant for the Titicut Separate Church in 1748. It is thoroughly Calvinistic and advocates paedo-baptism. Seven years later, after becoming a Baptist, Backus performed the same service for the First Baptist Church at Middleborough. Though the latter document advocates believers' baptism, it maintains the same Calvinistic stance which is found in the earlier confession (at times, employing identical language). For example, he affirms in the Baptist document, "4. That God who is Infinite in knowledge and perfectly views all things from

For example, the first covenant of the Separate Baptist Sandy Creek church contained strong affirmations of predestination, effectual calling, and perseverance of the saints. The preamble states:

> Holding believers' baptism; laying on of hands; *particular election of grace by predestination of God in Christ*; effectual calling by the Holy Ghost; free justification through the imputed righteousness of Christ; progressive sanctification through God's grace and truth; the final perseverance, or continuance of the saints in grace…[emphasis added].[28]

When the Sandy Creek Association adopted their *Articles of Faith* in 1816, the decidedly Calvinistic Basil Manly, Sr., chaired the committee that wrote them. It is not surprising, then, to read in Article III:

> That Adam fell from his original state of purity, and that his sin is imputed to his posterity; that human nature is corrupt,

the Beginning to the end of Time hath foreordained that whatsoever comes to pass, either by his Order or Permission shall Work for the eternal Glory of his Great Name" and "9. God the father of his mear (sic) good pleasure from all Eternity hath Chosen a number of poor, Lost men, in Christ Jesus to eternal Salvation." See Backus *Diary*, 3:1529–32, 1588–92.

[28] George Washington Paschal, *History of North Carolina Baptists* (Raleigh, NC: The General Board of North Carolina Baptist State Convention, 1930), 1:401. Paschal doubts, without justification, those records which attribute this covenant, including the preamble, to Shubal Stearns. See also William Lumpkin, *Baptist Foundations in the South* (Nashville, TN: Broadman Press, 1961), 36 and McBeth, *The Baptist Heritage*, 229.

and that man, of his own free will and ability, is impotent to regain the state in which he was primarily placed.

Also in Article IV:

We believe in election from eternity, effectual calling by the Holy Spirit of God, and justification in his sight only by the imputation of Christ's righteousness. And we believe that they who are thus elected, effectually called, and justified, will persevere through grace to the end, that none of them be lost.[29]

Here we have four of the five points of Calvinism stated and affirmed by the Separate Baptists of North Carolina. This is consistent with the report that David Benedict gives of the unification of Regular and Separate Baptists in Virginia in 1787. During the negotiations, the Separates assured the Regulars that, although they had never formally adopted a full confession of faith, the large majority of them nevertheless believed the Regular Baptist confession just as strongly as did the Regulars themselves.[30]

Even more telling are the doctrinal commitments that were embedded in the foundation of churches that Separate Baptists planted in Georgia. The Kiokee Baptist Church was planted by Daniel Marshall in 1772. The covenant that the church adopted at its founding opens with these unequivocal words:

[29] Purefoy, *A History*, 104–5.

[30] David Benedict, *A General History of the Baptist Denomination in America*, (Boston, MA: Manning & Loring, 1813), 60–62; quoted in McBeth, *A Sourcebook for The Baptist Heritage* (Nashville, TN: Broadman Press, 1990), 164–65.

According to God's appointment in His Word, we do hereby in His name and strength covenant and promise to keep up and defend all the articles of faith, according to God's Word, such as the great doctrine of election, effectual calling, particular redemption, justification by the imputed righteousness of Christ alone, sanctification by the spirit of God, believers' baptism by immersion, the saints' absolute final perseverance in grace, the resurrection of the dead, future rewards and punishments, etc., all according to Scripture which we take as the rule of our faith and practice, with some other doctrines herein not mentioned, as are commanded and supported by that blessed Book: denying the Arian, Socinian, and Arminian errors, and every other principle contrary to the Word of God. Now yet since we are exhorted to prove all things, orderly ministers of any denomination may when invited, preach in our meeting house.[31]

These doctrinal commitments are representative of those held by churches that formed the Georgia Baptist Association in 1784.

3. Leading Separate Baptist pastors were Calvinists

Not all Separate Baptist pastors were convinced Calvinists, but many of their most prominent pastors were. The Separate Baptist commitment to Reformed theology is clearly evident

---

[31] Timothy and Denise George, editors, *Baptist Confessions, Covenants and Catechisms* (Nashville, TN: Broadman and Holman, 1996), 205–6. This statement was revised in 1826 concerning how members were received and dismissed. See Thomas Ray, *Memoirs of Daniel and Abraham Marshall, Pioneer Baptist Evangelists to the South*, expanded and illustrated edition (Springfield, MO: Particular Baptist Press, 2006), 24.

in the expressed convictions of leaders such as Shubal Stearns, Daniel Marshall and his son, Abraham, Richard Furman and Isaac Backus.[32] The latter, in 1797, near the end of his life, wrote:

> The enmity which men have discovered against the sover-
> eignty of the grace of God as revealed in Holy Scriptures
> hath now prevailed so far that every art is made use of to put
> other senses upon the words of revelation than God intended
> therein. He said to Moses, "I will have mercy on whom I will
> have mercy, and I will have compassion on whom I will have
> compassion. So then it is not of him that willeth, nor of him
> that runneth, but of God that showeth mercy," Rom. 9:15–16.
> This was the doctrine that God made use of in all the ref-
> ormation that wrought in Germany, England and Scotland
> after the year 1517; and by the same doctrine he wrought all
> the reformation that has been in our day, both in Europe and
> America.[33]

The church covenant from the Kiokee Baptist church demonstrates that the founding pastor, Daniel Marshall, was convinced of the doctrines of grace. Inspired by the impassioned
preaching of George Whitefield, Marshall became a Presbyte-

---

[32] McLoughlin says of Stearns that "his style of preaching did much to set the tone of the new evangelical Calvinism of the reviv-al that broke out in Virginia and North Carolina" (Backus, *Diary*, 3:1248). Tom Nettles has described Furman as a "staunch Calvinist" (*By His Grace and For His Glory*, [Cape Coral, FL: Founders Press, 2006], xxxix).

[33] Alvah Hovey, *A Memoir of the Life and Times of Isaac Backus* (1858; reprint edition, Harrisonburg, VA: Gano Books, 1991), 356; quoted in Iain H. Murray, *Revival & Revivalism: The Making and Marring of American Evangelicalism 1750–1858* (Edinburgh, The Ban-ner of Truth Trust, 1994), 181–82.

rian missionary to the Mohawk Indians along the Susquehanna River in Pennsylvania. When hostilities among various tribes forced his removal from that work, he settled near Winchester, Virginia and began worshiping with a Baptist church that belonged to the Philadelphia Association. His son, Abraham, writes that only after "a close and impartial examination of their faith and order" (which certainly would have included the *Philadelphia Confession of Faith*) did he and his wife submit to baptism.[34]

Abraham himself was instrumental in writing the first articles of faith for the Georgia Baptist Association of churches in 1790. Called the "Abstract and Decorum," the articles reflect the Calvinism of the *Philadelphia Confession*.

> 3d. We believe in the fall of Adam, and the imputation of his sin to his posterity. In the corruption of human nature, and the impotency of man to recover himself by his own free will—ability.

> 4th. We believe in the everlasting love of God to his people, and the eternal election of a definite number of the human race, to grace and glory: And that there was a covenant of grace or redemption made between the Father and the Son, before the world began, in which their salvation is secure, and that they in particular are redeemed.

> 5th. We believe that sinners are justified in the sight of God, only by the righteousness of Christ imputed to them.

[34] Jesse Mercer, *A History of the Georgia Baptist Association* (Washington, GA: NP, 1838; reprint edition, 1979), 371.

6th. We believe that all those who were chosen in Christ, will be effectually called, regenerated, converted, sanctified, and supported by the spirit and power of God, so that they shall persevere in grace, and not one of them be finally lost.[35]

The three associations—Philadelphia, Charleston, and Sandy Creek—that were largely responsible for the spread of Baptist work throughout the South in the eighteenth and nineteenth centuries were all consciously devoted to Reformational Christianity. That is, they all adopted confessions of faith that affirm the basic tenets of the Protestant and Reformed view of salvation. In the case of Philadelphia and Charleston, the confession of faith was essentially the *Second London Confession* of 1689, the most Reformed of all the major Baptist confessions. Through these streams Southern Baptists trace our heritage. What they teach us is that many of the roots of our biblical convictions extend all the way back to that great movement of God in the sixteenth century known as the Protestant Reformation.

Conclusion

The evidence that has been presented clearly demonstrates that Southern Baptists come from Reformation stock. For all of the important distinctives that separate us from the leading Protestant Reformers, Baptists owe a debt of gratitude to God for those faithful leaders of the sixteenth century. With all of their shortcomings, they were nevertheless used of God to return to the Scripture alone for their authority. By doing so they

[35] Ray, *Memoirs*, 247–48.

rediscovered the blessed gospel of God—that gospel that reveals salvation by grace alone through faith alone in Christ alone and brings glory to God alone. To this, surely, every Southern Baptist can say, "Amen!"

When those 293 delegates registered in Augusta, Georgia, in May, 1845 to form a new denomination, they came with a united commitment to the reformational doctrines of God's sovereign grace in salvation. The churches and associations that they represented consciously held to a Reformed or Calvinistic understanding of salvation. One notable example is Patrick Hues Mell. In addition to being one of the original delegates who founded the Southern Baptist Convention, Mell went on to become one of the most influential leaders that the denomination has ever produced. He served as President of the Southern Baptist Convention for seventeen years.

In 1851 The Southern Baptist Publication Society published Mell's "concise and popular exposition" of the doctrines of grace.[36] He produced this work not only to refute some attacks by a non-Baptist writer, but also to counteract what he saw as some tendencies toward Arminianism among his Baptist brethren.[37]

Mell's concern for sound doctrine determined the character of his pastoral ministry. Mrs. D. B. Fitzgerald, one of the long-

---

[36] Mell, *A Southern Baptist Looks at Predestination* (Cape Coral, FL: Christian Gospel Foundation, n.d.), 15. This is a reprint of the original work which was entitled, *Predestination and the Saints Perseverance State and Defended* (Charleston, SC: The Southern Baptist Publication Society, 1851). The material in this book first appeared as a series of articles in the *Christian Index*, the Baptist paper of Georgia.

[37] Mell, *A Southern Baptist Looks at Predestination*, 15–16.

time members of the Antioch Baptist Church in Oglethorpe, Georgia, where Mell served as pastor, described his initial efforts at the church with the following words:

> When first called to take charge of the church Dr. Mell found it in a sad state of confusion. He said a number of the members were drifting off into Arminianism. He loved the truth too well to blow hot and cold with the same breath. It was a Baptist church and it must have doctrines peculiar to that denomination preached to it. And with that boldness, clearness, and vigor of speech that marked him, he preached to them the doctrines of predestination, election, free-grace, etc. He said it was always his business to preach the truth as he found it in God's Word, and leave the matter there, feeling that God would take of the results.[38]

This testimony is the spiritual and doctrinal heritage of the Southern Baptist Convention. Recent years have witnessed a growing revival of this heritage in our day. With the return to the authority of God's Word, such an outcome is inevitable. In a sense, this renewal is nothing less than a doctrinal homecoming for Southern Baptists. It is a return to the faith of our fathers. And if what our Baptist and Southern Baptist forefathers believed was true in their day, it is still true today—the Bible has not changed, God has not changed, and truth has not changed.

This revival is not something to be feared by those who do not understand it or who disagree with its theology. All Bible believing Southern Baptists will readily acknowledge that the vast majority of our churches are in need of spiritual revitaliza-

[38] P. H. Mell, Jr., *Life of Patrick Hues Mell* (Louisville, KY: Baptist Book Concern, 1895), 58–59.

tion. When the unregenerate members of our churches far out-number the regenerate ones, something is terribly wrong. When most of our 16.3 million members never even attend a church worship service on Sunday, it is obvious that we have problems. When only a small fraction of our churches even attempt to practice discipline anymore, it is time for us to wake up and admit that we need help.[39]

My prayer is that the Lord is in the process of sending help by calling us back to the healthier streams of biblical Christianity that characterized earlier generations of Southern Baptist life. Theological nicknames are not important. Neither is "winning" a doctrinal debate. In fact, my hope is that no Southern Baptist will try to coerce another to "dot every 'i' and cross every 't'" on the fine points of theology. Such efforts are unhealthy and distracting. What we need—what we absolutely must have—is a return to the apostolic doctrine and practice of the New Testament.

If this happens then Jesus Christ will regain His rightful place of supremacy in all our preaching and ministry. Churches will become increasingly gospel-driven with fresh understanding of and wonder at the sovereignty of God in salvation and providence. In many respects, this will result in churches and ministries becoming more closely aligned with those doctrines that have historically been nicknamed, "Calvinism." While it does not matter one bit whether or not that designation is used,

[39] An admission of these problems was finally made in a resolution that the 2008 Southern Baptist Convention passed in Indianapolis, Indiana. Resolution #6, "On Regenerate Church Membership and Church Member Restoration," available at:

http://www.sbc.net/resolutions/amResolution.asp?ID=1189

those who understand the historical background of the term need not be embarrassed by it.

I like what that great nineteenth-century Southern Baptist statesman John A. Broadus said about this matter. When he was traveling through Switzerland, gazing at the majestic Alps, he wrote the following in a letter that was published in the *Western Recorder*:

> The people who sneer at what is called Calvinism might as well sneer at Mont Blanc. We are not in the least bound to defend all of Calvin's opinions or actions, but I do not see how anyone who really understands the Greek of the Apostle Paul or the Latin of Calvin and Turretin can fail to see that these latter did but interpret and formulate substantially what the former teaches.... Whatever the inspired writers meant to teach is authoritative, the truth of God.[40]

What does Geneva have to do with Nashville? Precisely this: The biblical doctrines of God's grace which were expounded so clearly in the former are the theological heritage of the denomination whose main offices are located in the latter. So you may legitimately refer to those in our denomination who are returning to this heritage as "Calvinists." Or you may call them "Reformed" in their theology. Whatever label one uses, it should be remembered that this resurgence of the doctrines of grace is a recovery of the doctrinal heritage of the SBC.

[40] *Life and Letters of John A. Broadus*, (American Baptist Publication Society, 1901; reprint edition, Harrisonburg, VA: Gano Books, 1987), 396–97.

Appendix 1:
The Charleston
Confession of Faith

A Confession of Faith

Put forth

By the Elders and Brethren

of Many Congregations of Christians

(Baptized upon Profession of Their Faith)

In London and the Country

Adopted by the Baptist Association of Charleston, 1767

CHARLESTON EDTION

To which is added—an Article

on singing Psalms in Public Worship

With the heart man believeth unto righteousness and with the mouth confession is made unto salvation.—Romans X.10.

Search the Scriptures.—John V.39.

Charleston, (S.C.)

50

To the *Judicious* and *Impartial* Reader

Courteous Reader,

It is now many years since divers of us (with other sober Christians then living and walking in the way of the Lord that we profess) did conceive ourselves to be under a necessity of publishing a *Confession of our Faith*, for the information, and satisfaction of those, that did not thoroughly understand what our principles were, or had entertained prejudices against our profession, by reason of the strange representation of them, by some men of note, who had taken very wrong measures, and accordingly led others into misapprehensions, of us, and them: and this was first put forth about the year, 1643, in the name of seven Congregations then gathered in London; since which time, diverse impressions thereof have been dispersed abroad, and our end proposed, in good measure answered, inasmuch as many (and some of those men eminent, both for piety and learning) were thereby satisfied, that we were no way guilty of those heterodoxies and fundamental errors, which had too frequently been charged upon us without ground, or occasion given on our part. And forasmuch, as that *Confession* is not now commonly to be had; and also that many others have since embraced the same truth which is owned therein; it was judged necessary by us to join together in giving a testimony to the world; of our firm adhering to those wholesome principles, by the publication of this which is now in your hand.

And forasmuch as our method, and manner of expressing our sentiments, in this, does vary from the former (although the substance of the matter is the same) we shall freely impart to you the reason and occasion thereof. One thing that greatly prevailed with us to undertake this work, was (not only to give a full account of ourselves, to those Christians that differ from us about the subject of baptism, but also) the profit that might from thence arise, unto those that have any account of our labors, in their instruction, and establishment in the great truths of the Gospel; in the clear understanding, and steady belief of which, our comfortable walking with God, and fruitfulness before Him, in all our ways, is most nearly concerned; and therefore we did conclude it necessary to express ourselves the more fully, and distinctly; and also to fix on such a method as might be most comprehensive of those things which we designed to explain our sense, and belief of; and finding no defect, in this regard, in that fixed on by the assembly, and after them by those of the congregational way, we did readily conclude it best to retain the same *order* in our present Confession: and also, when we observed that those last mentioned, did in their confession (for reasons which seemed of weight both to themselves and others) choose not only to express their mind in words concurrent with the former in sense, concerning all those articles wherein they were agreed, but also for the most part without any variation of the terms we did in like manner conclude it best to follow their example in making use of the very same words with them both, in these articles (which are very many) wherein our faith and doctrine is the same with theirs, and this we did, the more abundantly, to manifest our consent with both, in all the fundamental articles of the Christian religion, as also with many others, whose orthodox confessions have been published to the world; on behalf of the Protestants in divers nations and cities: and also to convince all, that we have no itch to clog Religion with new words, but do readily acquiesce in that form of sound words, which hath been, in consent with the holy Scriptures, used by others before us;

hereby declaring before God, angels, and men, our hearty agreement with them, in that wholesome Protestant Doctrine, which with so clear evidence of Scriptures they have asserted: some things indeed, are in some places added, some terms omitted, and some few changed, but these alterations are of that nature, as that we need not doubt, any charge or suspicion of unsoundness in the faith, from any of our brethren upon the account of them.

In those things wherein we differ from others, we have expressed ourselves with all candor and plainness that none might entertain jealousy of ought secretly lodged in our breasts, that we would not the world should be acquainted with; yet we hope we have also observed those rules of modesty, and humility, as will render our freedom in this respect inoffensive, even to those whose sentiments are different from ours.

We have also taken care to affix texts of Scripture, at the bottom, for the confirmation of each article in our confession; in which work we have studiously endeavored to select such as are most clear and pertinent, for the proof of what is asserted by us: and our earnest desire is, that all into whose hands this may come, would follow that (never enough commended) example of the noble *Bereans*, who searched the Scriptures daily, that they might find out whether the things preached to them were so or not.

There is one thing more which we sincerely profess, and earnestly desire credence in, viz. That contention is most remote from our design in all that we have done in this matter: and we hope the liberty of an ingenuous unfolding our principles, and opening our hearts unto our brethren, with the Scripture grounds of our faith and practice, will by none of them be either denied to us, or taken ill from us. Our whole design is accomplished, if we may obtain that justice, as to be measured in our principles, and practice, and the judgment of both by others, according to what we have now published; which the Lord (whose eyes are as a flame of fire) knows to be the doctrine, which with our hearts we must firmly believe, and sincerely endeavor to conform our lives to. And Oh! that other contentions being laid asleep, the only care and contention of all upon whom the name of our blessed Redeemer is called, might for the future be, to walk humbly with their God, and in the exercise of all Love and Meekness towards each other, to perfect holiness in the fear of the Lord, each one endeavoring to have his conversation such as becomes the Gospel; and also suitable to his place and capacity vigorously to promote in others the practice of true Religion and undefiled in the sight of God and our Father. And that in this backsliding day, we might not spend our breath in fruitless complaints of the evils of others; but may every one begin at home, to reform in the first place our own hearts, and ways; and then to quicken all that we may have influence upon, to the same work; that if the will of God were so, none might deceive themselves, by resting in, and trusting to, a form of godliness, without the power of it, and inward experience of the efficacy of those truths that are professed by them.

And verily there is one spring and cause of the decay of religion in our day, which we cannot but touch upon, and earnestly urge a redress of; and that is the neglect of the worship of God in families, by those to whom the charge and conduct of them is committed. May not the gross ignorance, and instability of many; with the profaneness of others, be justly charged upon their parents and masters; who have not trained them up in the way wherein they ought to walk when they were young: but have neglected those frequent and solemn commands which the

Lord has laid upon them so to catechize, and instruct them, that their tender years might be seasoned with the knowledge of the truth of God as revealed in the Scriptures; and also by their own omission of prayer, and other duties of religion in their families, together with the ill example of their loose conversation, have inured them first to a neglect, and then contempt of all piety and religion? We know this will not excuse the blindness, or wickedness of any; but certainly it will fall heavy upon those that have thus been the occasion thereof; they indeed dye in their sins; but will not their blood be required of those under whose care they were, who yet permitted them to go on without warning, yea led them into the paths of destruction? And will not the diligence of Christians with respect to the discharge of these duties, in ages past, rise up in judgment against, and condemn many of those who would be esteemed such now?

We shall conclude with our earnest prayer, that the God of all grace, will pour out those measures of His Holy Spirit upon us, that the profession of truth may be accompanied with the sound belief, and diligent practice of it by us; that His name may in all things be glorified, through Jesus Christ our Lord, *Amen*.

I. Of the Holy Scriptures

1:1 The Holy Scripture is the only sufficient, certain, and infallible rule of all saving knowledge, faith, and obedience [a]. Although the light of nature, and the works of creation and providence do so far manifest the goodness, wisdom, and power of God, as to leave men inexcusable; yet they are not sufficient to give that knowledge of God and His will which is necessary unto salvation [b]. Therefore it pleased the Lord at sundry times and in divers manners to reveal Himself, and to declare His will unto His church; [c] and afterward for the better preserving and propagating of the truth, and for the more sure establishment and comfort of the church against the corruption of the flesh, and the malice of Satan, and of the world, to commit the same wholly unto writing; which makes the Holy Scriptures to be most necessary, those former ways of God's revealing His will unto His people being now ceased [d].

[a] 2 Timothy 3:15–17; Isaiah 8:20; Luke 16:29,31; Ephesians 2:20
[b] Romans 1:19–21, 2:14,15; Psalm 19:1–3 [c] Hebrews 1:1
[d] Proverbs 22:19–21; Romans 15:4; 2 Peter 1:19,20

1:2 Under the name of Holy Scripture, or the Word of God written, are now contained all the books of the Old and New Testaments, which are these:

OF THE OLD TESTAMENT:
      Genesis
      Exodus
      Leviticus
      Numbers

Deuteronomy
Joshua
Judges
Ruth
1 Samuel
2 Samuel
1 Kings
2 Kings
1 Chronicles
2 Chronicles
Ezra
Nehemiah
Ester
Job
Psalms
Proverbs
Ecclesiastes
The Song of Solomon
Isaiah
Jeremiah
Lamentations
Ezekiel
Daniel
Hosea
Joel
Amos
Obadiah
Jonah
Micah
Nahum
Habakkuk

Zephaniah
Haggai
Zechariah
Malachi

OF THE NEW TESTAMENT:

Matthew
Mark
Luke
John
The Acts of the Apostles
Paul's Epistle to the Romans
1 Corinthians
2 Corinthians
Galatians
Ephesians
Philippians
Colossians
1 Thessalonians
2 Thessalonians
1 Timothy
2 Timothy
Titus
Philemon
The Epistle to the Hebrews
Epistle of James
The 1st and 2nd Epistles of Peter
The 1st, 2nd and 3rd Epistles of John
The Epistle of Jude
The Revelation

1

All of which are given by the inspiration of God, to be the rule of faith and life [e].

[e] 2 Timothy 3:16

1:3 The books commonly called Apocrypha, not being of divine inspiration, are no part of the canon (or rule) of the Scripture, and, therefore, are of no authority to the church of God, nor to be any otherwise approved or made use of than other human writings [f].

[f] Luke 24:27,44; Romans 3:2

1:4 The authority of the Holy Scripture, for which it ought to be believed, depends not upon the testimony of any man or church, but wholly upon God (who is truth itself), the author thereof; therefore it is to be received because it is the Word of God [g].

[g] 2 Peter 1:19–21; 2 Timothy 3:16; 2 Thessalonians 2:13; 1 John 5:9

1:5 We may be moved and induced by the testimony of the church of God to a high and reverent esteem of the Holy Scriptures; and the heavenliness of the matter, the efficacy of the doctrine, and the majesty of the style, the consent of all the parts, the scope of the whole (which is to give all glory to God), the full discovery it makes of the only way of man's salvation, and many other incomparable excellencies, and entire perfections thereof, are arguments whereby it does abundantly evidence itself to be the Word of God; yet notwithstanding, our full persuasion and assurance of the infallible truth, and divine authority thereof, is from the inward work of the Holy Spirit bearing witness by and with the Word in our hearts [h].

[h] John 16:13,14; 1 Corinthians 2:10–12; 1 John 2:20,27

1:6 The whole counsel of God concerning all things necessary for His own glory, man's salvation, faith and life, is either expressly set down or necessarily contained in the Holy Scripture; unto which nothing at any time is to be added, whether by new revelation of the Spirit, or traditions of men [i]. Nevertheless, we acknowledge the inward illumination of the Spirit of God to be necessary for the saving understanding of such things as are revealed in the Word, [k] and that there are some circumstances concerning the worship of God, and government of the church, common to human actions and societies, which are to be ordered by the light of nature and Christian prudence, according to the general rules of the Word, which are always to be observed [l].

[i] 2 Timothy 3:15–17; Galatians 1:8,9 [k] John 6:45; 1 Corinthians 2:9–12 [l] 1 Corinthians 11:13,14; 14:26,40

1:7 All things in Scripture are not alike plain in themselves, nor alike clear unto all; [m] yet those things which are necessary to be known, believed and observed for salvation, are so clearly propounded and opened in some place of Scripture or other, that not only the learned, but the unlearned, in a due use of ordinary means, may attain to a sufficient understanding of them [n].

[m] 2 Peter 3:16 [n] Psalm 19:7; 119:130

1:8 The Old Testament in Hebrew (which was the native language of the people of God of old), [o] and the New Testament in Greek (which at the time of the writing of it was most generally known to the nations), being immediately inspired by God, and by His singular care and providence kept pure in all ages, are therefore authentic; so as in all controversies of religion, the church is finally to appeal to them [p]. But because these original tongues are not known to all the people of God, who have a right unto, and interest in the Scriptures, and are commanded in the fear of God to read, [q] and search them, [r] therefore they are to be translated into the vulgar language of every nation unto which they come, [s] that the Word of God dwelling plentifully in all, they may worship Him in an acceptable manner, and through patience and comfort of the Scriptures may have hope [t].

[o] Romans 3:2 [p] Isaiah 8:20 [q] Acts 15:15 [r] John 5:39
[s] 1 Corinthians 14:6,9,11,12,24,28 [t] Colossians 3:16

1:9 The infallible rule of interpretation of Scripture is the Scripture itself; and therefore when there is a question about the true and full sense of any Scripture (which is not manifold, but one), it must be searched by other places that speak more clearly [u].

[u] 2 Peter 1:20, 21; Acts 15:15,16

1:10 The supreme judge, by which all controversies of religion are to be determined, and all decrees of councils, opinions of ancient writers, doctrines of men, and private spirits, are to be examined, and in whose sentence we are to rest, can be no other but the Holy Scripture delivered by the Spirit, into which Scripture so delivered, our faith is finally resolved [x].

[x] Matthew 22:29,31,32; Ephesians 2:20; Acts 28:23

II. Of God and of the Holy Trinity

2:1 The Lord our God is but one only living and true God; [a] whose subsistence is in and of Himself, [b] infinite in being and perfection; whose essence cannot be comprehended by any but Himself; [c] a most pure spirit, [d] invisible, without body, parts, or passions, who only has immortality, dwelling in the light which no man can approach unto; [e] who is immutable, [f] immense, [g] eternal, [h] incomprehensible, almighty, [i] every way infinite, most holy, [k] most wise, most free, most absolute; working all things according to the counsel of His own immutable and most righteous will, [l] for His own glory; [m] most loving, gracious, merciful, long-suffering, abundant in goodness and truth, forgiving iniquity, transgression and sin; the rewarder of them that diligently seek Him, [n] and withal most just and terrible in His judgments, [o] hating all sin, [p] and will by no means clear the guilty [q].

[a] 1 Corinthians 8:4,6; Deuteronomy 6:4 [b] Jeremiah 10:10; Isaiah 48:12 [c] Exodus 3:14 [d] John 4:24 [e] 1 Timothy 1:17; Deuteronomy 4:15,16 [f] Malachi 3:6 [g] 1 Kings 8:27; Jeremiah 23:23 [h] Psalm 90:2 [i] Genesis 17:1 [k] Isaiah 6:3 [l] Psalm 115:3; Isaiah 46:10 [m] Proverbs 16:4; Romans 11:36 [n] Exodus 34:6,7; Hebrews 11:6 [o] Nehemiah 9:32,33 [p] Psalm 5:5,6 [q] Exodus 34:7; Nahum 1:2,3

2:2 God, having all life, [r] glory, [s] goodness, [t] blessedness, in and of Himself, is alone in and unto Himself all-sufficient, not standing in need of any creature which He has made, nor deriving any glory from them, [u] but only manifesting His own glory in, by, unto, and upon them; He is the alone fountain of all being, of whom, through whom, and to whom are all things, [x] and He has most sovereign dominion over all creatures, to do by them, for them, or upon them, whatsoever Himself pleases; [y] in His sight all things are open and manifest, [z] His knowledge is infinite, infallible, and independent upon the creature, so as nothing is to Him contingent or uncertain; [a] He is most holy in all His counsels, in all His works, [b] and in all His commands; to Him is due from angels and men, whatsoever worship, [c] service, or obedience, as creatures they owe unto the Creator, and whatever He is further pleased to require of them.

[r] John 5:26 [s] Psalm 148:13 [t] Psalm 119:68 [u] Job 22:2,3
[x] Romans 11:34–36 [y] Daniel 4:25,34,35 [z] Hebrews 4:13
[a] Ezekiel 11:5; Acts 15:18 [b] Psalm 145:17 [c] Revelation 5:12–14

2:3 In this divine and infinite Being there are three subsistences, the Father, the Word (or Son), and Holy Spirit, [d] of one substance, power, and eternity, each having the whole divine essence, yet the essence undivided: [e] the Father is of one, neither begotten nor proceeding; the Son is eternally begotten of the Father; [f] the Holy Spirit proceeding from the Father and the Son; [g] all infinite, without beginning, therefore but one God, who is not to be divided in nature and being, but distinguished by several peculiar relative properties and personal relations;

which doctrine of the Trinity is the foundation of all our communion with God, and comfortable dependence on Him.

[d] 1 John 5:7; Matthew 28:19; 2 Corinthians 13:14 [e] Exodus 3:14; John 14:11; 1 Corinthians 8:6 [f] John 1:14,18 [g] John 15:26; Galatians 4:6

III. Of God's Decree

3:1 God has decreed in Himself, from all eternity, by the most wise and holy counsel of His own will, freely and unchangeably, all things, whatsoever comes to pass; [a] yet so as thereby is God neither the author of sin nor has fellowship with any therein; [b] nor is violence offered to the will of the creature, nor yet is the liberty or contingency of second causes taken away, but rather established; [c] in which appears His wisdom in disposing all things, and power and faithfulness in accomplishing His decree [d].

[a] Isaiah 46:10; Ephesians 1:11; Hebrews 6:17; Romans 9:15,18
[b] James 1:15,17; 1 John 1:5 [c] Acts 4:27,28; John 19:11
[d] Numbers 23:19; Ephesians 1:3–5

3:2 Although God knows whatsoever may or can come to pass, upon all supposed conditions, [e] yet has He not decreed anything, because He foresaw it as future, or as that which would come to pass upon such conditions [f].

[e] Acts 15:18 [f] Romans 9:11,13,16,18

3:3 By the decree of God, for the manifestation of His glory, some men and angels are predestinated, or foreordained to eternal life through Jesus Christ, [g] to the praise of His glorious grace; [h] others being left to act in their sin to their just condemnation, to the praise of His glorious justice [i].

[g] 1 Timothy 5:21; Matthew 25:34 [h] Ephesians 1:5,6
[i] Romans 9:22,23; Jude 4

3:4 These angels and men thus predestinated and foreordained, are particularly and unchangeably designed, and their number so certain and definite, that it cannot be either increased or diminished [k].

[k] 2 Timothy 2:19; John 13:18

3:5 Those of mankind that are predestinated to life, God, before the foundation of the world was laid, according to His eternal and immutable purpose, and the secret counsel and good pleasure of His will, has chosen in Christ unto everlasting glory, out of His mere free grace and love, [l] without any other thing in the creature as a condition or cause moving Him thereunto [m].

[l] Ephesians 1:4, 9, 11; Romans 8:30; 2 Timothy 1:9; 1 Thessalonians 5:9 [m] Romans 9:13,16; Ephesians 2:9,12

3:6 As God has appointed the elect unto glory, so He has, by the eternal and most free purpose of His will, foreordained all the means thereunto; [n] wherefore they who are elected, being fallen in Adam, are redeemed by Christ, [o] are effectually called unto faith in Christ, by His Spirit working in due season, are justified, adopted, sanctified, [p] and kept by His power through faith unto salvation; [q] neither are any other redeemed by Christ, or effectually called, justified, adopted, sanctified, and saved, but the elect only [r].

[n] 1 Peter 1:2; 2 Thessalonians 2:13 [o] 1 Thessalonians 5:9,10
[p] Romans 8:30; 2 Thessalonians 2:13 [q] 1 Peter 1:5 [r] John 10:26, 17:9, 6:64

3:7 The doctrine of this high mystery of predestination is to be handled with special prudence and care, that men attending the will of God revealed in His Word, and yielding obedience thereunto, may, from the certainty of their effectual vocation, be assured of their eternal election; [s] so shall this doctrine afford matter of praise, [t] reverence, and admiration of God, and of humility, [u] diligence, and abundant consolation to all that sincerely obey the gospel [x]

[s] 1 Thessalonians 1:4,5; 2 Peter 1:10 [t] Ephesians 1:6; Romans 11:33 [u] Romans 11:5,6,20 [x] Luke 10:20

IV. Of Creation

4:1 In the beginning it pleased God the Father, Son, and Holy Spirit, [a] for the manifestation of the glory of His eternal power, [b] wisdom, and goodness, to create or make the world, and all things therein, whether visible or invisible, in the space of six days, and all very good [c].

[a] John 1:1–3; Hebrews 1:2; Job 26:13 [b] Romans 1:20 [c] Colossians 1:16; Genesis 1:31

4:2 After God had made all other creatures, He created man, male and female, [d] with reasonable and immortal souls, [e] rendering them fit unto that life to God for which they were created; being made after the image of God, in knowledge, righteousness, and true holiness; [f] having the law of God written in their hearts, [g] and power to fulfill it, and yet under a possibility of transgressing, being left to the liberty of their own will, which was subject to change [h].

[d] Genesis 1:27 [e] Genesis 2:7 [f] Ecclesiastes 7:29; Genesis 1:26
[g] Romans 2:14,15 [h] Genesis 3:6

4:3 Besides the law written in their hearts, they received a command not to eat of the tree of knowledge of good and evil, [i] which while they kept, they were happy in their communion with God, and had dominion over the creatures [k].

[i] Genesis 2:17; 3:8–12 [k] Genesis 1:26,28

V. Of Divine Providence

5:1 God the good Creator of all things, in His infinite power and wisdom does uphold, direct, dispose, and govern all creatures and things, [a] from the greatest even to the least, [b] by His most wise and holy providence, to the end for the which they were created, according unto His infallible foreknowledge, and the free and immutable counsel of His own will; to the praise of the glory of His wisdom, power, justice, infinite goodness and mercy [c].

[a] Hebrews 1:3; Job 38:11; Isaiah 46:10,11; Psalm 135:6
[b] Matthew 10:29–31 [c] Ephesians 1:11

5:2 Although in relation to the foreknowledge and decree of God, the first cause, all things come to pass immutably and infallibly; [d] so that there is not anything befalls any by chance, or without His providence; [e] yet by the same providence He ordered them to fall out according to the nature of second causes, either necessarily, freely, or contingently [f].

[d] Acts 2:23 [e] Proverbs 16:33 [f] Genesis 8:22

5:3 God, in His ordinary providence makes use of means, [g] yet is free to work without, [h] above, [i] and against them [k] at His pleasure.

[g] Acts 27:31,44; Isaiah 55:10,11 [h] Hosea 1:7 [i] Romans 4:19–21 [k] Daniel 3:27

5:4 The almighty power, unsearchable wisdom, and infinite goodness of God, so far manifest themselves in His providence, that His determinate counsel extends itself even to the first fall, and all other sinful actions both of angels and men; [l] and that not by a bare permission, which also He most wisely and powerfully bounds, and otherwise orders and governs, [m] in a manifold dispensation to His most holy ends; [n] yet so, as the sinfulness of their acts proceeds only from the creatures, and not from God, who, being most holy and righteous, neither is nor can be the author or approver of sin [o].

[l] Romans 11:32–34; 2 Samuel 24:1; 1 Chronicles 21:1
[m] 2 Kings 19:28; Psalm 76:10 [n] Genesis 1:20; Isaiah 10:6,7,12
[o] Psalm 50:21; 1 John 2:16

5:5 The most wise, righteous, and gracious God does often times leave for a season His own children to manifold temptations and the corruptions of their own hearts, to chastise them for their former sins, or to discover unto them the hidden strength of corruption and deceitfulness of their hearts, that they may be humbled; and to raise them to a more close and constant dependence for their support upon Himself; and to make them more watchful against all future occasions of sin, and for other just and holy ends [p]. So that whatsoever befalls any of His elect is by His appointment, for His glory, and their good [q].

[p] 2 Chronicles 32:25,26,31; 2 Samuel 24:1; 2 Corinthians 12:7–9
[q] Romans 8:28

5:6 As for those wicked and ungodly men whom God, as the righteous judge, for former sin does blind and harden; [r] from them He not only withholds His grace, whereby they might have been enlightened in their understanding, and wrought upon in their hearts; [s] but sometimes also withdraws the gifts which they had, [t] and exposes them to such objects as their corruptions make occasion of sin; [u] and withal, gives them over to their own lusts, and the temptations of the world, and the power of Satan, [x] whereby it comes to pass that they harden themselves, even under those means which God uses for the softening of others [y].

[r] Romans 1;24–28, 11:7,8 [s] Deuteronomy 29:4 [t] Matthew 13:12 [u] Deuteronomy 2:30; 2 Kings 8:12,13 [x] Psalm 81:11,12; 2 Thessalonians 2:10–12 [y] Exodus 8:15,32; Isaiah 6:9,10; 1 Peter 2:7,8

5:7 As the providence of God does in general reach to all creatures, so after a more special manner it takes care of His church, and disposes of all things to the good thereof [z].

[z] 1 Timothy 4:10; Amos 9:8,9; Isaiah 43:3–5

VI. Of the Fall of Man, of Sin, And of the Punishment Thereof

6:1 Although God created man upright and perfect, and gave him a righteous law, which had been unto life had he kept it, and threatened death upon the breach thereof, [a] yet he did not long abide in this honor; Satan using the subtlety of the serpent to subdue Eve, then by her seducing Adam, who, without any compulsion, did willfully transgress the law of their creation, and the command given unto them, in eating the forbidden fruit, [b] which God was pleased, according to His wise and holy counsel to permit, having purposed to order it to His own glory.

[a] Genesis 2:16,17 [b] Genesis 3:12,13; 2 Corinthians 11:3

6:2 Our first parents, by this sin, fell from their original righteousness and communion with God, and we in them, whereby death came upon all: [c] all becoming dead in sin, [d] and wholly defiled in all the faculties and parts of soul and body [e].

[c] Romans 3:23 [d] Romans 5:12, etc. [e] Titus 1:15; Genesis 6:5; Jeremiah 17:9; Romans 3:10–19

6:3 They being the root, and by God's appointment, standing in the room and stead of all mankind, the guilt of the sin was imputed, and corrupted nature conveyed, to all their posterity descending from them by ordinary generation, [f] being now conceived in sin, [g] and by nature children of wrath, [h] the servants of sin, the subjects of death, [i] and all other miseries, spiritual, temporal and eternal, unless the Lord Jesus set them free [k].

[f] Romans 5:12–19; 1 Corinthians 15:21,22,45,49 [g] Psalm 51:5; Job 14:4 [h] Ephesians 2:3 [i] Romans 6:20, 5:12 [k] Hebrews 2:14,15; 1 Thessalonians 1:10

6:4 From this original corruption, whereby we are utterly indisposed, disabled, and made opposite to all good, and wholly inclined to all evil, [l] do proceed all actual transgressions [m].

[l] Romans 8:7; Colossians 1:21 [m] James 1:14,15; Matthew 15:19

6:5 The corruption of nature, during this life, does remain in those that are regenerated; [n] and although it be through Christ pardoned and mortified, yet both itself, and the first motions thereof, are truly and properly sin [o].

[n] Romans 7:18,23; Ecclesiastes 7:20; 1 John 1:8 [o] Romans 7:24–25; Galatians 5:17

VII. Of God's Covenant

7:1 The distance between God and the creature is so great, that although reasonable creatures do owe obedience to Him as their creator, yet they could never have attained the reward of life but by some voluntary condescension on God's part, which He has been pleased to express by way of covenant [a].

[a] Luke 17:10; Job 35:7,8

7:2 Moreover, man having brought himself under the curse of the law by his fall, it pleased the Lord to make a covenant of grace, [b] wherein He freely offers unto sinners life and salvation by Jesus Christ, requiring of them faith in Him, that they may be saved; [c] and promising to give unto all those that are ordained unto eternal life, His Holy Spirit, to make them willing and able to believe [d].

[b] Genesis 2:16,17; Galatians 3:10; Romans 3:20,21 [c] Romans 8:3; Mark 16:15,16; John 3:16; [d] Ezekiel 36:26,27; John 6:44,45; Psalm 110:3

7:3 This covenant is revealed in the gospel; and was first of all to Adam in the promise of salvation by the seed of the woman, [e] and afterwards by farther steps, until the full discovery thereof was completed in the New Testament; [f] and it is founded in that eternal covenant transaction that was between the Father and the Son about the redemption of the elect; [g] and it is alone by the grace of this covenant that all the posterity of fallen Adam that ever were saved did obtain life and blessed immortality, man being now utterly incapable of acceptance with God upon those terms on which Adam stood in his state of innocency [h].

[e] Genesis 3:15 [f] Hebrews 1:1 [g] 2 Timothy 1:9; Titus 1:2
[h] Hebrews 11:6,13; Romans 4:1,2, etc.; Acts 4:12; John 8:56

VIII. Of Christ the Mediator

8:1 It pleased God, in His eternal purpose, to choose and ordain the Lord Jesus, His only begotten Son, according to the covenant made between them both, to be the mediator between God and man; [a] the prophet, [b] priest, [c] and king; [d] head and Savior of His church, [e] the heir of all things, [f] and judge of the world; [g] unto whom He did from all eternity give a people to be His seed and to be by Him in time redeemed, called, justified, sanctified, and glorified [h].

[a] Isaiah 42:1; 1 Peter 1:19,20 [b] Acts 3:22 [c] Hebrews 5:5,6
[d] Psalm 2:6; Luke 1:33 [e] Ephesians 1:22,23 [f] Hebrews 1:2
[g] Acts 17:31 [h] Isaiah 53:10; John 17:6; Romans 8:30

8:2 The Son of God, the second person in the Holy Trinity, being very and eternal God, the brightness of the Father's glory, of one substance and equal with Him who made the world, who upholds and governs all things He has made, did, when the fullness of time was complete, take upon Him man's nature, with all the essential properties and common infirmities thereof, [i] yet without sin; [k] being conceived by the Holy Spirit in the womb of the Virgin Mary, the Holy Spirit coming down upon her: and the power of the Most High overshadowing her; and so was made of a woman of the tribe of Judah, of the seed of Abraham and David according to the Scriptures; [l] so that two whole, perfect, and distinct natures were inseparably joined together in one person, without conversion, composition, or confusion; which person is very God and very man, yet one Christ, the only mediator between God and man [m].

[i] John 1:14; Galatians 4:4 [k] Romans 8:3; Hebrews 2:14–17, 4:15 [l] Matthew 1:22,23; Luke 1:27,31,35 [m] Romans 9:5; 1 Timothy 2:5

8:3 The Lord Jesus, in His human nature thus united to the divine, in the person of the Son, was sanctified and anointed with the Holy Spirit above measure, [n] having in Him all the treasures of wisdom and knowledge; [o] in whom it pleased the Father that all fullness should dwell, [p] to the end that being holy, harmless, undefiled, [q] and full of grace and truth, [r] He might be thoroughly furnished to execute the office of mediator and surety; [s] which office He took not upon Himself, but was thereunto called by His Father; [t] who also put all power and judgment in His hand, and gave Him commandment to execute the same [u].

[n] Psalm 45:7; Acts 10:38; John 3:34 [o] Colossians 2:3 [p] Colossians 1:19 [q] Hebrews 7:26 [r] John 1:14 [s] Hebrews 7:22 [t] Hebrews 5:5 [u] John 5:22,27; Matthew 28:18; Acts 2:36

8:4 This office the Lord Jesus did most willingly undertake, [x] which that He might discharge He was made under the law, [y] and did perfectly fulfill it, and underwent the punishment due to us, which we should have born and suffered, [z] being made sin and a curse for us; [a] enduring most grievous sorrows in His soul, and most painful sufferings in His body; [b] was crucified, and died, and remained in the state of the dead, yet saw no corruption: [c] on the third day He arose from the dead [d] with

74

the same body in which He suffered, [e] with which He also ascended into heaven, [f] and there sits at the right hand of His Father making intercession, [g] and shall return to judge men and angels at the end of the world [h].

[x] Psalm 40:7,8; Hebrews 10:5–10; John 10:18 [y] Galatians 4:4; Matthew 3:15 [z] Galatians 3:13; Isaiah 53:6; 1 Peter 3:18 [a] 2 Corinthians 5:21 [b] Matthew 26:37,38; Luke 22:44; Matthew 27:46 [c] Acts 13:37 [d] 1 Corinthians 15:3,4 [e] John 20:25,27 [f] Mark 16:19; Acts 1:9–11 [g] Romans 8:34; Hebrews 9:24 [h] Acts 10:42; Romans 14:9,10; Acts 1:11; 2 Peter 2:4

8:5 The Lord Jesus, by His perfect obedience and sacrifice of Himself, which He through the eternal Spirit once offered up to God, has fully satisfied the justice of God, [i] procured reconciliation, and purchased an everlasting inheritance in the kingdom of heaven, for all those whom the Father has given unto Him [k].

[i] Hebrews 9:14, 10:14; Romans 3:25,26 [k] John 17:2; Hebrews 9:15

8:6 Although the price of redemption was not actually paid by Christ until after His incarnation, yet the virtue, efficacy, and benefit thereof were communicated to the elect in all ages, successively from the beginning of the world, in and by those promises, types, and sacrifices wherein He was revealed, and signified to be the seed which should bruise the serpent's head; [l] and the Lamb slain from the foundation of the world, [m] being the same yesterday, and today and forever [n].

[l] 1 Corinthians 4:10; Hebrews 4:2; 1 Peter 1:10,11 [m] Revelation 13:8 [n] Hebrews 13:8

8:7 Christ, in the work of mediation, acts according to both natures, by each nature doing that which is proper to itself; yet by reason of the unity of the person, that which is proper to one nature is sometimes in Scripture, attributed to the person denominated by the other nature [o].

[o] John 3:13; Acts 20:28

8:8 To all those for whom Christ has obtained eternal redemption, He does certainly and effectually apply and communicate the same, making intercession for them; [p] uniting them to Himself by His Spirit, revealing to them, in and by His Word, the mystery of salvation, persuading them to believe and obey, [q] governing their hearts by His Word and Spirit, [r] and overcoming all their enemies by His almighty power and wisdom, [s] in such manner and ways as are most consonant to His wonderful and unsearchable dispensation; and all of free and absolute grace, without any condition foreseen in them to procure it [t].

[p] John 6:37, 10:15,16, 17:9; Romans 5:10 [q] John 17:6; Ephesians 1:9; 1 John 5:20 [r] Romans 8:9,14 [s] Psalm 110:1; 1 Corinthians 15:25,26 [t] John 3:8; Ephesians 1:8

8:9 This office of mediator between God and man is proper only to Christ, who is the prophet, priest, and king of the church of God; and may not be either in whole, or any part thereof, transferred from Him to any other [u].

[u] 1 Timothy 2:5

8:10 This number and order of offices is necessary; for in respect of our ignorance, we stand in need of His prophetical office; [x] and in respect of our alienation from God, and imperfection of the best of our services, we need His priestly office to reconcile us and present us acceptable unto God; [y] and in respect to our averseness and utter inability to return to God, and for our rescue and security from our spiritual adversaries, we need His kingly office to convince, subdue, draw, uphold, deliver, and preserve us to His heavenly kingdom [z].

[x] John 1:18 [y] Colossians 1:21; Galatians 5:17 [z] John 16:8; Psalm 110:3; Luke 1:74,75

IX. Of Free Will

9:1 God has endued the will of man with that natural liberty and power of acting upon choice, that it is neither forced, nor by any necessity of nature determined to do good or evil [a].

[a] Matthew 17:12; James 1:14; Deuteronomy 30:19

9:2 Man, in his state of innocency, had freedom and power to will and to do that which was good and well-pleasing to God, [b] but yet was unstable, so that he might fall from it [c].

[b] Ecclesiastes 7:29 [c] Genesis 3:6

9:3 Man, by his fall into a state of sin, has wholly lost all ability of will to any spiritual good accompanying salvation; [d] so as a natural man, being altogether averse from that good, and dead in sin, [e] is not able by his own strength to convert himself, or to prepare himself thereunto [f].

[d] Romans 5:6, 8:7 [e] Ephesians 2:1,5 [f] Titus 3:3–5; John 6:44

9:4 When God converts a sinner, and translates him into the state of grace, He frees him from his natural bondage under sin, [g] and by His grace alone enables him freely to will and to do that which is spiritually good; [h] yet so as that by reason of his remaining corruptions, he does not perfectly, nor only will that which is good, but does also will that which is evil [i].

[g] Colossians 1:13; John 8:36 [h] Philippians 2:13 [i] Romans 7:15,18,19,21,23

9:5 This will of man is made perfectly and immutably free to good alone in the state of glory only [k].

[k] Ephesians 4:13

X. Of Effectual Calling

10:1 Those whom God has predestinated unto life, He is pleased in His appointed, and accepted time, effectually to call, [a] by His Word and Spirit, out of that state of sin and death in which they are by nature, to grace and salvation by Jesus Christ; [b] enlightening their minds spiritually and savingly to understand the things of God; [c] taking away their heart of stone, and giving to them a heart of flesh; [d] renewing their wills, and by His almighty power determining them to that which is good, and effectually drawing them to Jesus Christ; [e] yet so as they come most freely, being made willing by His grace [f].

[a] Romans 8:30, 11:7; Ephesians 1:10,11; 2 Thessalonians 2:13,14
[b] Ephesians 2:1–6 [c] Acts 26:18; Ephesians 1:17,18 [d] Ezekiel
36:26 [e] Deuteronomy 30:6; Ezekiel 36:27; Ephesians 1:19
[f] Psalm 110:3; Canticles 1:4

10:2 This effectual call is of God's free and special grace alone, not from anything at all foreseen in man, nor from any power or agency in the creature co-working with His special grace, [g] the creature being wholly passive therein, being dead in sins and trespasses, until being quickened and renewed by the Holy Spirit; [h] he is thereby enabled to answer this call, and to embrace the grace offered and conveyed in it, and that by no less power than that which raised up Christ from the dead [i].

[g] 2 Timothy 1:9; Ephesians 2:8 [h] 1 Corinthians 2:14; Ephesians 2:5; John 5:25; [i] Ephesians 1:19,20

10:3 Elect infants dying in infancy are regenerated and saved by Christ through the Spirit; [k] who works when, and where, and how He pleases; [l] so also are all other elect persons, who are incapable of being outwardly called by the ministry of the Word.

[k] John 3:3, 5, 6 [l] John 3:8

10:4 Others not elected, although they may be called by the ministry of the Word, and may have some common operations of the Spirit, [m] yet not being effectually drawn by the Father, they neither will nor can truly come to Christ, and therefore cannot be saved: [n] much less can men that do not receive the Christian religion be saved; be they never so diligent to frame their lives according to the light of nature and the law of that religion they do profess [o].

[m] Matthew 22:14, 13:20,21; Hebrews 6:4,5 [n] John 6:44,45,65; 1 John 2:24,25 [o] Acts 4:12; John 4:22, 17:3

XI. Of Justification

11:1 Those whom God effectually calls, He also freely justifies, [a] not by infusing righteousness into them, but by pardoning their sins, and by accounting and accepting their persons as righteous; [b] not for anything wrought in them, or done by them, but for Christ's sake alone; [c] not by imputing faith itself, the act of believing, or any other evangelical obedience to them, as their righteousness; but by imputing Christ's active obedience unto the whole law, and passive obedience in His death for their whole and sole righteousness, [d] they receiving and resting on Him and His righteousness by faith, which faith they have not of themselves; it is the gift of God [e].

[a] Romans 3:24; 8:30 [b] Romans 4:5–8, Ephesians 1:7
[c] 1 Corinthians 1:30,31, Romans 5:17–19 [d] Philippians 3:8,9;
Ephesians 2:8–10 [e] John 1:12; Romans 5:17

11:2. Faith thus receiving and resting on Christ and His righteousness, is the alone instrument of justification; [f] yet is not alone in the person justified, but is ever accompanied with all other saving graces, and is no dead faith, but works by love [g].

[f] Romans 3:28 [g] Galatians 5:6, James 2:17,22,26

11:3 Christ, by His obedience and death, did fully discharge the debt of all those that are justified; and did, by the sacrifice of Himself in the blood of his cross, undergoing in their stead the penalty due unto them, make a proper, real, and full satisfaction to God's justice in their behalf; [h] yet, in as much as He was given by the Father for them, and His obedience and satisfaction accepted in their stead, and both freely, not for anything in them, [i] their justification is only of free grace, that both the exact justice and rich grace of God might be glorified in the justification of sinners [k].

[h] Hebrews 10:14; 1 Peter 1:18,19; Isaiah 53:5,6 [i] Romans 8:32; 2 Corinthians 5:21 [k] Romans 3:26; Ephesians 1:6,7, 2:7

11:4 God did from all eternity decree to justify all the elect, [l] and Christ did in the fullness of time die for their sins, and rise again for their justification; [m] nevertheless, they are not justified personally, until the Holy Spirit does in due time actually apply Christ unto them [n].

[l] Galatians 3:8, 1 Peter 1:2, 1 Timothy 2:6 [m] Romans 4:25
[n] Colossians 1:21,22, Titus 3:4–7

11:5 God does continue to forgive the sins of those that are justified, [o] and although they can never fall from the state of justification, [p] yet they may, by their sins, fall under God's fatherly displeasure; [q] and in that condition they have not usually the light of His countenance restored unto them, until they humble themselves, confess their sins, beg pardon, and renew their faith and repentance [r].

[o] Matthew 6:12, 1 John 1:7,9 [p] John 10:28 [q] Psalm 89:31–33
[r] Psalm 32:5; 51:7–12; Matthew 26:75

11:6 The justification of believers under the Old Testament was, in all these respects, one and the same with the justification of believers under the New Testament [s].

[s] Galatians 3:9; Romans 4:22–24

XII. Of Adoption

12:1 All those that are justified, God vouchsafed, in and for the sake of His only Son Jesus Christ, to make partakers of the grace of adoption, [a] by which they are taken into the number, and enjoy the liberties and privileges of children of God, [b] have His name put on them, [c] receive the spirit of adoption, [d] have access to the throne of grace with boldness, are enabled to cry Abba, Father, [e] are pitied, [f] protected, [g] provided for, [h] and chastened by Him as by a Father, [i] yet never cast off, [k] but sealed to the day of redemption, [l] and inherit the promises as heirs of everlasting salvation [m].

[a] Ephesians 1:5; Galatians 4:4,5 [b] John 1:12; Romans 8:17 [c] 2 Corinthians 6:18; Revelation 3:12 [d] Romans 8:15 [e] Galatians 4:6; Ephesians 2:18 [f] Psalm 103:13 [g] Proverbs 14:26 [h] 1 Peter 5:7 [i] Hebrews 12:6 [k] Isaiah 54:8,9; Lamentations 3:31 [l] Ephesians 4:30 [m] Hebrews 1:14, 6:12

XIII. Of Sanctification

13:1 They who are united to Christ, effectually called, and regenerated, having a new heart and a new spirit created in them through the virtue of Christ's death and resurrection, are also

82

farther sanctified, really and personally, [a] through the same virtue, by His Word and Spirit dwelling in them; [b] the dominion of the whole body of sin is destroyed, [c] and the several lusts thereof are more and more weakened and mortified, [d] and they more and more quickened and strengthened in all saving graces, [e] to the practice of all true holiness, without which no man shall see the Lord [f].

[a] Acts 20:32; Romans 6:5,6 [b] John 17:17; Ephesians 3:16–19; 1 Thessalonians 5:21–23 [c] Romans 6:14 [d] Galatians 5:14, 24 [e] Colossians 1:11 [f] 2 Corinthians 7:1; Hebrews 12:14

13:2 This sanctification is throughout in the whole man, [g] yet imperfect in this life; there abides still some remnants of corruption in every part, [h] whence arises a continual and irreconcilable war; the flesh lusting against the spirit, and the spirit against the flesh [i].

[g] 1 Thessalonians 5:23 [h] Romans 7:18, 23 [i] Galatians 5:17; 1 Peter 2:11

13:3 In which war, although the remaining corruption for a time may much prevail, [k] yet, through the continual supply of strength from the sanctifying Spirit of Christ, the regenerate part does overcome; [l] and so the saints grow in grace, perfecting holiness in the fear of God, pressing after an heavenly life, in evangelical obedience to all the commands which Christ as Head and King, in His Word has prescribed to them [m].

[k] Romans 7:23 [l] Romans 6:14 [m] Ephesians 4:15,16; 2 Corinthians 3:18, 7:1

XIV. Of Saving Faith

14:1 The grace of faith, whereby the elect are enabled to believe to the saving of their souls, is the work of the Spirit of Christ in their hearts, [a] and is ordinarily wrought by the ministry of the Word; [b] by which also, and by the administration of baptism and the Lord's supper, prayer, and other means appointed of God, it is increased and strengthened [c].

[a] 2 Corinthians 4:13; Ephesians 2:8 [b] Romans 10:14,17
[c] Luke 17:5; 1 Peter 2:2; Acts 20:32

14:2 By this faith a Christian believes to be true whatsoever is revealed in the Word on the authority of God Himself, [d] and also apprehends an excellency therein above all other writings and all things in the world, [e] as it bears forth the glory of God in His attributes, the excellency of Christ in His nature and offices, and the power and fullness of the Holy Spirit in His workings and operations: and so is enabled to cast his soul upon the truth thus believed, [f] and also acts differently upon that which each particular passage thereof contains; yielding obedience to the commands, [g] trembling at the threatenings, [h] and embracing the promises of God for this life and that which is to come; [i] but the principle acts of saving faith have immediate relation to Christ, accepting, receiving, and resting upon Him alone for justification, sanctification, and eternal life, by virtue of the covenant of grace [k].

[d] Acts 24:14 [e] Psalm 19:7–10, 119:72 [f] 2 Timothy 1:12
[g] John 15:14 [h] Isaiah 66:2 [i] Hebrews 11:13 [k] John 1:12;
Acts 16:31; Galatians 2:20; Acts 15:11

14:3 This faith, although it be in different degrees, and may be weak or strong, [l] yet it is in the least degree of it different in the kind or nature of it (as is all other saving grace) from the faith and common grace of temporary believers; [m] and therefore, though it may be many times assailed and weakened, yet it gets the victory, [n] growing up in many to the attainment of a full assurance through Christ, [o] who is both the author and finisher of our faith [p].

[l] Hebrews 5:13,14; Matthew 6:30; Romans 4:19,20 [m] 2 Peter 1:1 [n] Ephesians 6:16; 1 John 5:4,5 [o] Hebrews 6:11,12; Colossians 2:2 [p] Hebrews 12:2

XV. Of Repentance unto Life and Salvation

15:1 Such of the elect that are converted at riper years, having for sometime lived in the state of nature, and therein served divers pleasures, God in their effectual calling gives them repentance unto life [a].

[a] Titus 3:2–5

15:2 Whereas there is none that does good and sins not, [b] and the best of men may, through the power and deceitfulness of their corruption dwelling in them, with the prevalency of temptation, fall into greater sins and provocations; God has in the covenant of grace, mercifully provided that believers so sinning and falling be renewed through repentance unto salvation [c].

[b] Ecclesiastes 7:20 [c] Luke 22:31,32

15:3 This saving repentance is an evangelical grace, [d] whereby a person, being by the Holy Spirit made sensible of the manifold evils of his sin, does, by faith in Christ, humble himself for it, with godly sorrow, detestation of it, and self-abhorrancy, [e] praying for pardon and strength of grace, with a purpose and endeavor, by supplies of the Spirit, to walk before God unto all well-pleasing in all things [f].

[d] Zechariah 12:10; Acts 11:18 [e] Ezekiel 36:31; 2 Corinthians 7:11 [f] Psalm 119:6,128

15:4 As repentance is to be continued through the whole course of our lives, upon the account of the body of death, and the motions thereof, so it is every man's duty to repent of his particular known sins particularly [g].

[g] Luke 19:8; 1 Timothy 1:13,15

15:5 Such is the provision which God has made through Christ in the covenant of grace for the preservation of believers unto salvation, that although there is no sin so small but it deserves damnation, [h] yet there is no sin so great that it shall bring damnation on them that repent, [i] which makes the constant preaching of repentance necessary.

[h] Romans 6:23 [i] Isaiah 1:16–18, 55:7

XVI. Of Good Works

16:1 Good works are only such as God has commanded in His Holy Word, [a] and not such as without the warrant thereof are devised by men out of blind zeal, or upon any pretense of good intentions [b].

[a] Micah 6:8; Hebrews 13:21 [b] Matthew 15:9; Isaiah 29:13

16:2 These good works, done in obedience to God's commandments, are the fruits and evidences of a true and lively faith; [c] and by them believers manifest their thankfulness, [d] strengthen their assurance, [e] edify their brethren, adorn the profession of the gospel, [f] stop the mouths of the adversaries, and glorify God, [g] whose workmanship they are, created in Christ Jesus thereunto, [h] that having their fruit unto holiness they may have the end eternal life [i].

[c] James 2:18,22 [d] Psalm 116:12,13 [e] 1 John 2:3,5; 2 Peter 1:1–11 [f] Matthew 5:16 [g] 1 Timothy 6:1; 1 Peter 2:15; Philippians 1:11 [h] Ephesians 2:10 [i] Romans 6:22

16:3 Their ability to do good works is not at all of themselves, but wholly from the Spirit of Christ; [k] and that they may be enabled thereunto, besides the graces they have already received, there is necessary an actual influence of the same Holy Spirit, to work in them and to will and to do of his good pleasure; [l] yet they are not hereupon to grow negligent, as if they were not bound to perform any duty, unless upon a special motion of the

Spirit, but they ought to be diligent in stirring up the grace of God that is in them [m].

[k] John 15:4,5 [l] 2 Corinthians 3:5; Philippians 2:13 [m] Philippians 2:12; Hebrews 6:11,12; Isaiah 64:7

16:4. They who in their obedience attain to the greatest height which is possible in this life, are so far from being able to super-erogate, and to do more than God requires, as that they fall short of much which in duty they are bound to do [n].

[n] Job 9:2,3; Galatians 5:17; Luke 17:10

16:5 We cannot by our best works merit pardon of sin or eternal life at the hand of God, by reason of the great disproportion that is between them and the glory to come, and the infinite distance that is between us and God, whom by them we can neither profit nor satisfy for the debt of our former sins; [o] but when we have done all we can, we have done but our duty, and are unprofitable servants; and because as they are good they proceed from His Spirit, [p] and as they are wrought by us they are defiled and mixed with so much weakness and imperfection, that they cannot endure the severity of God's judgment [q].

[o] Romans 3:20; Ephesians 2:8,9; Romans 4:6 [p] Galatians 5:22,23 [q] Isaiah 64:6; Psalm 143:2

16:6 Yet notwithstanding the persons of believers being accepted through Christ, their good works also are accepted in Him; [r] not as though they were in this life wholly unblamable and unreprovable in God's sight, but that He, looking upon them in

His Son, is pleased to accept and reward that which is sincere, although accompanied with many weaknesses and imperfection [s].

[r] Ephesians 1:5; 1 Peter 2:5 [s] Matthew 25:21,23; Hebrews 6:10

16:7 Works done by unregenerate men, although for the matter of them they may be things which God commands, and of good use both to themselves and others; [t] yet because they proceed not from a heart purified by faith, [u] nor are done in a right manner according to the Word, [w] nor to a right end, the glory of God, [x] they are sinful and cannot please God, nor make a man meet to receive grace from God, [y] and yet their neglect of them is more sinful and displeasing to God [z].

[t] 2 Kings 10:30; 1 Kings 21:27,29 [u] Genesis 4:5; Hebrews 11:4,6 [w] 1 Corinthians 13:1 [x] Matthew 6:2,5 [y] Amos 5:21,22; Romans 9:16; Titus 3:5 [z] Job 21:14,15; Matthew 25:41–43

XVII. Of the Perseverance of the Saints

17:1 Those whom God has accepted in the beloved, effectually called and sanctified by His Spirit, and given the precious faith of His elect unto, can neither totally nor finally fall from the state of grace, but shall certainly persevere therein to the end, and be eternally saved, seeing the gifts and callings of God are without repentance, whence He still begets and nourishes in them faith, repentance, love, joy, hope, and all the graces of the Spirit unto immortality; [a] and though many storms and floods arise and beat against them, yet they shall never be able to take them off that foundation and rock which by faith they are fastened upon; notwithstanding, through unbelief and the temptations of Satan, the sensible sight of the light and love of God may for a time be clouded and obscured from them, [b] yet He is still the same, and they shall be sure to be kept by the power of God unto salvation, where they shall enjoy their purchased possession, they being engraven upon the palm of His hands, and their names having been written in the book of life from all eternity [c].

[a] John 10:28,29; Philippians 1:6; 2 Timothy 2:19; 1 John 2:19
[b] Psalm 89:31,32; 1 Corinthians 11:32 [c] Malachi 3:6

17:2 This perseverance of the saints depends not upon their own free will, but upon the immutability of the decree of election, [d] flowing from the free and unchangeable love of God the Father, upon the efficacy of the merit and intercessions of Jesus Christ and union with Him, [e] the oath of God, [f] the abiding of His Spirit, and the seed of God within them, [g] and the nature of the covenant of grace; [h] from all which arises also the certainty and infallibility thereof.

[d] Romans 8:30, 9:11,16 [e] Romans 5:9,10; John 14:19
[f] Hebrews 6:17,18 [g] 1 John 3:9 [h] Jeremiah 32:40

17:3 And though they may, through the temptation of Satan and of the world, the prevalency of corruption remaining in them, and the neglect of means of their preservation, fall into grievous sins, and for a time continue therein; [i] whereby they incur God's displeasure and grieve His Holy Spirit, [k] come to have their graces and comforts impaired, [l] have their hearts hardened, and their consciences wounded, [m] hurt and scandalize others, and bring temporal judgments upon themselves, [n] yet they shall renew their repentance and be preserved through faith in Christ Jesus to the end [o].

[i] Matthew 26:70,72,74 [k] Isaiah 64:5,9; Ephesians 4:30
[l] Psalm 51:10,12 [m] Psalm 32:3,4 [n] 2 Samuel 12:14
[o] Luke 22:32,61,62

XVIII. Of the Assurance of Grace and Salvation

18:1 Although temporary believers and other unregenerate men, may vainly deceive themselves with false hopes and carnal presumptions of being in the favor of God and in a state of salvation, which hope of theirs shall perish; [a] yet such as truly believe in the Lord Jesus, and love Him in sincerity, endeavoring to walk in all good conscience before Him, may in this life be certainly assured that they are in the state of grace, and may rejoice in the hope of the glory of God, [b] which hope shall never make them ashamed [c].

[a] Job 8:13,14; Matthew 7:22,23 [b] 1 John 2:3, 3:14,18,19,21,24, 5:13 [c] Romans 5:2,5

18:2 This certainty is not a bare conjectural and probable persuasion grounded upon a fallible hope, but an infallible assurance of faith, [d] founded on the blood and righteousness of Christ revealed in the Gospel; [e] and also upon the inward evidence of those graces of the Spirit unto which promises are made, [f] and on the testimony of the Spirit of adoption, witnessing with our spirits that we are the children of God; [g] and as a fruit thereof, keeping the heart both humble and holy [h].

[d] Hebrews 6:11,19 [e] Hebrews 6:17,18 [f] 2 Peter 1:4,5,10,11
[g] Romans 8:15,16 [h] 1 John 3:1–3

18:3 This infallible assurance does not so belong to the essence of faith, but that a true believer may wait long, and conflict with many difficulties before he be partaker of it; [i] yet being enabled by the Spirit to know the things which are freely given him of God, he may, without extraordinary revelation, in the right use of means, attain thereunto: [k] and therefore it is the duty of every one to give all diligence to make his calling and election sure, that thereby his heart may be enlarged in peace and joy in the Holy Spirit, in love and thankfulness to God, and in strength and cheerfulness in the duties of obedience, the proper fruits of this assurance; [l]—so far is it from inclining men to looseness [m].

[i] Isaiah 50:10; Psalm 88; Psalm 77:1–12 [k] 1 John 4:13;
Hebrews 6:11,12 [l] Romans 5:1,2,5, 14:17; Psalm 119:32
[m] Romans 6:1,2; Titus 2:11,12,14

18:4 True believers may have the assurance of their salvation divers ways shaken, diminished, and intermitted; as by negligence in preserving of it, [n] by falling into some special sin which wounds the conscience and grieves the Spirit; [o] by some sudden or vehement temptation, [p] by God's withdrawing the light of His countenance, and suffering even such as fear Him to walk in darkness and to have no light, [q] yet are they never destitute of the seed of God [r] and life of faith, [s] that love of

Christ and the brethren, that sincerity of heart and conscience of duty out of which, by the operation of the Spirit, this assurance may in due time be revived, [t] and by the which, in the meantime, they are preserved from utter despair [u].

[n] Canticles 5:2,3,6 [o] Psalm 51:8,12,14 [p] Psalm 116:11; 77:7,8, 31:22 [q] Psalm 30:7 [r] 1 John 3:9 [s] Luke 22:32
[t] Psalm 42:5,11 [u] Lamentations 3:26–31

XIX. Of the Law of God

19:1 God gave to Adam a law of universal obedience written in his heart, and a particular precept of not eating the fruit of the tree of knowledge of good and evil; [a] by which He bound him and all his posterity to personal, entire, exact, and perpetual obedience; [b] promised life upon the fulfilling, and threatened death upon the breach of it, and endued him with power and ability to keep it [c].

[a] Genesis 1:27; Ecclesiastes 7:29 [b] Romans 10:5 [c] Galatians 3:10,12

19:2 The same law that was first written in the heart of man continued to be a perfect rule of righteousness after the fall, [d] and was delivered by God upon Mount Sinai, in ten commandments, and written in two tables, the four first containing our duty towards God, and the other six, our duty to man [e].

[d] Romans 2:14,15 [e] Deuteronomy 10:4

19:3 Besides this law, commonly called moral, God was pleased to give to the people of Israel ceremonial laws, containing several typical ordinances, partly of worship, prefiguring Christ, His graces, actions, sufferings, and benefits; [f] and partly holding forth divers instructions of moral duties, [g] all which ceremonial laws being appointed only to the time of reformation, are, by Jesus Christ the true Messiah and only law-giver, who was furnished with power from the Father for that end abrogated and taken away [h].

[f] Hebrews 10:1; Colossians 2:17 [g] 1 Corinthians 5:7
[h] Colossians 2:14,16,17; Ephesians 2:14,16

19:4 To them also He gave sundry judicial laws, which expired together with the state of that people, not obliging any now by virtue of that institution; their general equity only being of moral use [i].

[i] 1 Corinthians 9:8–10

19:5 The moral law does for ever bind all, as well justified persons as others, to the obedience thereof, [k] and that not only in regard of the matter contained in it, but also in respect of the authority of God the Creator, who gave it; [l] neither does Christ in the Gospel any way dissolve, but much strengthen this obligation [m].

[k] Romans 13:8–10; James 2:8,10–12 [l] James 2:10,11
[m] Matthew 5:17–19; Romans 3:31

19:6 Although true believers be not under the law as a covenant of works, to be thereby justified or condemned, [n] yet it is of great use to them as well as to others, in that as a rule of life, informing them of the will of God and their duty, it directs and binds them to walk accordingly; discovering also the sinful pollutions of their natures, hearts, and lives, so as examining themselves thereby, they may come to further conviction of, humiliation for, and hatred against, sin; [o] together with a clearer sight of the need they have of Christ and the perfection of His obedience; it is likewise of use to the regenerate to restrain their corruptions, in that it forbids sin; and the threatenings of it serve to show what even their sins deserve, and what afflictions in this life they may expect for them, although freed from the curse and unallayed rigor thereof. The promises of it likewise show them God's approbation of obedience, and what blessings they may expect upon the performance thereof, though not as due to them by the law as a covenant of works; so as man's doing good and refraining from evil, because the law encourages to the one and deters from the other, is no evidence of his being under the law and not under grace [p].

[n] Romans 6:14; Galatians 2:16; Romans 8:1, 10:4 [o] Romans 3:20, 7:7, etc. [p] Romans 6:12–14; 1 Peter 3:8–13

19:7 Neither are the aforementioned uses of the law contrary to the grace of the Gospel, but do sweetly comply with it, [q] the Spirit of Christ subduing and enabling the will of man to do that freely and cheerfully which the will of God, revealed in the law, requires to be done [r].

[q] Galatians 3:21 [r] Ezekiel 36:27

XX. Of the Gospel and of the Extent of Grace Thereof

20:1 The covenant of works being broken by sin, and made unprofitable unto life, God was pleased to give forth the promise of

Christ, the seed of the woman, as the means of calling the elect, and begetting in them faith and repentance; [a] in this promise the gospel, as to the substance of it, was revealed, and [is] therein effectual for the conversion and salvation of sinners [b].

[a] Genesis 3:15 [b] Revelation 13:8

20:2 This promise of Christ, and salvation by Him, is revealed only by the Word of God; [c] neither do the works of creation or providence, with the light of nature, make discovery of Christ, or of grace by Him, so much as in a general or obscure way; [d] much less that men destitute of the revelation of Him by the promise or gospel, should be enabled thereby to attain saving faith or repentance [e].

[c] Romans 1:17 [d] Romans 10:14,15,17 [e] Proverbs 29:18;
Isaiah 25:7; 60:2,3

20:3 The revelation of the gospel unto sinners, made in divers times and by sundry parts, with the addition of promises and precepts for the obedience required therein, as to the nations and persons to whom it is granted, is merely of the sovereign will and good pleasure of God; [f] not being annexed by virtue of any promise to the due improvement of men's natural abilities, by virtue of common light received without it, which none ever did make, or can do so; [g] and therefore in all ages, the preaching of the gospel has been granted unto persons and nations, as to the extent or straitening of it, in great variety, according to the counsel of the will of God.

[f] Psalm 147:20; Acts 16:7 [g] Romans 1:18–32

20:4. Although the gospel be the only outward means of revealing Christ and saving grace, and is, as such, abundantly sufficient thereunto; yet that men who are dead in trespasses may be born again, quickened or regenerated, there is moreover necessary an effectual insuperable work of the Holy Spirit upon the whole soul, for the producing in them a new spiritual life; [h] without which no other means will effect their conversion unto God [i].

[h] Psalm 110:3; 1 Corinthians 2:14; Ephesians 1:19,20 [i] John 6:44; 2 Corinthians 4:4,6

XXI. Of Christian Liberty and Liberty of Conscience

21:1 The liberty which Christ has purchased for believers under the gospel, consists in their freedom from the guilt of sin, the condemning wrath of God, the severity and curse of the law, [a] and in their being delivered from this present evil world, [b] bondage to Satan, [c] and dominion of sin, [d] from the evil of afflictions, [e] the fear and sting of death, the victory of the grave, [f] and everlasting damnation: [g] as also in their free access to God, and their yielding obedience unto Him, not out of slavish fear, [h] but a child-like love and willing mind [i]. All which were common also to believers under the law for the substance of them; [k] but under the New Testament the liberty of Christians is further enlarged, in their freedom from the yoke of a ceremonial law, to which the Jewish church was subjected, and in greater boldness of access to the throne of grace, and in fuller communications of the free Spirit of God, than believers under the law did ordinarily partake of [l].

[a] Galatians 3:13 [b] Galatians 1:4 [c] Acts 26:18 [d] Romans 8:3 [e] Romans 8:28 [f] 1 Corinthians 15:54–57 [g] 2 Thessalonians

1:10 [h] Romans 8:15; [i] Luke 1:73–75; 1 John 4:18 [k] Galatians 3:9,14 [l] John 7:38,39; Hebrews 10:19–21

21:2 God alone is Lord of the conscience, [m] and has left it free from the doctrines and commandments of men which are in any thing contrary to His Word, or not contained in it [n]. So that to believe such doctrines, or obey such commands out of conscience, is to betray true liberty of conscience; [o] and the requiring of an implicit faith, an absolute and blind obedience, is to destroy liberty of conscience and reason also [p].

[m] James 4:12; Romans 14:4 [n] Acts 4:19,29; 1 Corinthians 7:23; Matthew 15:9 [o] Colossians 2:20,22,23 [p] 1 Corinthians 3:5; 2 Corinthians 1:24

21:3 They who upon pretence of Christian liberty do practice any sin, or cherish any sinful lust, as they do thereby pervert the main design of the grace of the gospel to their own destruction, [q] so they wholly destroy the end of Christian liberty, which is, that being delivered out of the hands of all our enemies, we might serve the Lord without fear, in holiness and righteousness before Him, all the days of our lives [r].

[q] Romans 6:1,2 [r] Galatians 5:13; 2 Peter 2:18,21

XXII. Of Religious Worship and the Sabbath Day

22:1 The light of nature shows that there is a God, who has lordship and sovereignty over all; is just, good and does good unto all; and is therefore to be feared, loved, praised, called upon, trusted in, and served, with all the heart and all the soul, and with all the might [a]. But the acceptable way of worshipping the true God, is instituted by Himself, [b] and so limited by His own revealed will, that He may not be worshipped according to the imagination and devices of men, nor the suggestions of Satan, under any visible representations, or any other way not prescribed in the Holy Scriptures [c].

[a] Jeremiah 10:7; Mark 12:33 [b] Deuteronomy 12:32 [c] Exodus 20:4–6

22:2 Religious worship is to be given to God the Father, Son, and Holy Spirit, and to Him alone; [d] not to angels, saints, or any other creatures; [e] and since the fall, not without a mediator, [f] nor in the mediation of any other but Christ alone [g].

[d] Matthew 4:9,10; John 6:23; Matthew 28:19 [e] Romans 1:25; Colossians 2:18; Revelation 19:10 [f] John 14:6 [g] 1 Timothy 2:5

22:3 Prayer, with thanksgiving, being one part of natural worship, is by God required of all men [h]. But that it may be accepted, it is to be made in the name of the Son, [i] by the help of the Spirit, [k] according to His will; [l] with understanding, reverence, humility, fervency, faith, love, and perseverance; and when with others, in a known tongue [m].

[h] Psalm 95:1–7, 65:2 [i] John 14:13,14 [k] Romans 8:26
[l] 1 John 5:14 [m] 1 Corinthians 14:16,17

22:4 Prayer is to be made for things lawful, and for all sorts of men living, or that shall live hereafter; [n] but not for the dead, [o] nor for those of whom it may be known that they have sinned the sin unto death [p].

[n] 1 Timothy 2:1,2; 2 Samuel 7:29 [o] 2 Samuel 12:21–23
[p] 1 John 5:16

22:5 The reading of the Scriptures, [q] preaching, and hearing the Word of God, [r] teaching and admonishing one another in psalms, hymns, and spiritual songs, singing with grace in our hearts to the Lord; [s] as also the administration of baptism, [t] and the Lord's supper, [u] are all parts of religious worship of God, to be performed in obedience to Him, with understanding, faith, reverence, and godly fear; moreover, solemn humiliation, with fastings, [x] and thanksgivings, upon special occasions, ought to be used in an holy and religious manner [y].

[q] 1 Timothy 4:13 [r] 2 Timothy 4:2; Luke 8:18 [s] Colossians 3:16; Ephesians 5:19 [t] Matthew 28:19,20 [u] 1 Corinthians 11:26 [x] Esther 4:16; Joel 2:12 [y] Exodus 15:1–19, Psalm 107

22:6 Neither prayer nor any other part of religious worship, is now under the gospel, tied unto, or made more acceptable by any place in which it is performed, or towards which it is directed; but God is to be worshipped everywhere in spirit and in truth; [z] as in private families [a] daily, [b] and in secret each one by himself; [c] so more solemnly in the public assemblies, which are not carelessly nor willfully to be neglected or forsaken, when God by His word or providence calls thereunto [d].

[z] John 4:21; Malachi 1:11; 1 Timothy 2:8 [a] Acts 10:2 [b] Matthew 6:11; Psalm 55:17 [c] Matthew 6:6 [d] Hebrews 10:25; Acts 2:42

22:7 As it is the law of nature, that in general a proportion of time, by God's appointment, be set apart for the worship of God, so by His Word, in a positive moral, and perpetual commandment, binding all men, in all ages, He has particularly appointed one day in seven for a sabbath to be kept holy unto Him, [e] which from the beginning of the world to the resurrection of

Christ was the last day of the week, and from the resurrection of Christ was changed into the first day of the week, which is called the Lord's Day: [f] and is to be continued to the end of the world as the Christian Sabbath, the observation of the last day of the week being abolished.

[e] Exodus 20:8 [f] 1 Corinthians 16:1,2; Acts 20:7; Revelation 1:10

22:8 The sabbath is then kept holy unto the Lord, when men, after a due preparing of their hearts, and ordering their common affairs aforehand, do not only observe a holy rest all day, from their own works, words and thoughts, about their worldly employment and recreations, [g] but are also taken up the whole time in the public and private exercises of His worship, and in the duties of necessity and mercy [h].

[g] Isaiah 58:13; Nehemiah 13:15–22 [h] Matthew 12:1–13

XXIII. Of Singing of Psalms in Public Worship

23:1 We believe that singing the praises of God, is a holy ordinance of Christ, and not a part of natural religion, or a moral duty only; but that it is brought under divine institution, it being enjoined on the Churches of Christ to sing psalms, hymns, and spiritual songs; [a] and that the whole church in their public assemblies (as well as private Christians) ought to sing God's praises according to the best light they have received [b]. Moreover, it was practiced in the great representative church, by our Lord Jesus Christ with His disciples, after He had instituted and celebrated the sacred ordinance of His holy supper, as a commemorative token of redeeming love [c].

[a] Acts 16:25; Ephesians 5:19; Colossians 3:16 [b] Hebrews 2:12; James 5:13 [c] Matthew 26:30; Mark 14:26

XXIV. Of Lawful Oaths and Vows

24:1 A lawful oath is a part of religious worship, wherein the person swearing in truth, righteousness, and judgment, solemnly calls God to witness what he swears, [a] and to judge him according to the truth or falseness thereof [b].

[a] Exodus 20:7; Deuteronomy 10:20; Jeremiah 4:2 [b] 2 Chronicles 6:22,23

24:2 The name of God only is that by which men ought to swear; and therein it is to be used, with all holy fear and reverence; therefore to swear vainly or rashly by that glorious and dreadful name, or to swear at all by any other thing, is sinful, and to be abhorred; [c] yet as in matter of weight and moment, for confirmation of truth, and ending all strife, an oath is warranted by the word of God; [d] so a lawful oath being imposed by lawful authority in such matters, ought to be taken [e].

[c] Matthew 5:34,37; James 5:12 [d] Hebrews 6:16; 2 Corinthians 1:23 [e] Nehemiah 13:25

24:3 Whosoever takes an oath warranted by the word of God, ought duly to consider the weightiness of so solemn an act, and therein to avouch nothing but what he knows to be truth; for that by rash, false, and vain oaths, the Lord is provoked, and for them this land mourns [f].

[f] Leviticus 19:12; Jeremiah 23:10

24:4 An oath is to be taken in the plain and common sense of the words, without equivocation or mental reservation [g].

[g] Psalm 24:4

24:5 A vow, which is not to be made to any creature, but to God alone, is to be made and performed with all religious care and faithfulness; [h] but popish monastical vows of perpetual single life, [i] professed poverty, [k] and regular obedience, are so far from being degrees of higher perfection, that they are superstitious and sinful snares, in which no Christian may entangle himself [l].

[h] Psalm 76:11; Genesis 28:20–22 [i] 1 Corinthians 7:2,9
[k] Ephesians 4:28 [l] Matthew 19:1

XXV. Of the Civil Magistrate

25:1 God, the supreme Lord and King of all the world, has ordained civil magistrates to be under Him, over the people, for His own glory and the public good; and to this end has armed them with the power of the sword, for defense and encouragement of them that do good, and for the punishment of evil doers [a].

[a] Romans 13:1–4

25:2. It is lawful for Christians to accept and execute the office of a magistrate when called thereunto; in the management whereof, as they ought especially to maintain justice and peace, [b] according to the wholesome laws of each kingdom and commonwealth, so for that end they may lawfully now, under the New Testament, wage war upon just and necessary occasions [c].

[b] 2 Samuel 23:3; Psalm 82:3,4 [c] Luke 3:14

25:3 Civil magistrates being set up by God for the ends aforesaid; subjection, in all lawful things commanded by them, ought to be yielded by us in the Lord, not only for wrath, but for conscience' sake; [d] and we ought to make supplications and prayers for kings and all that are in authority, that under them we may live a quiet and peaceable life, in all godliness and honesty [e].

[d] Romans 13:5–7; 1 Peter 2:17 [e] 1 Timothy 2:1,2

XXVI. Of Marriage

26:1 Marriage is to be between one man and one woman; neither is it lawful for any man to have more than one wife, nor for any woman to have more than one husband at the same time [a].

[a] Genesis 2:24; Malachi 2:15; Matthew 19:5,6

26:2. Marriage was ordained for the mutual help of husband and wife, [b] for the increase of mankind with a legitimate issue, [c] and the preventing of uncleanness [d].

[b] Genesis 2:18 [c] Genesis 1:28 [d] 1 Corinthians 7:2,9

26:3 It is lawful for all sorts of people to marry, who are able with judgment to give their consent; [e] yet it is the duty of Christians to marry in the Lord; [f] and therefore such as profess the true religion, should not marry with infidels, or idolaters; neither should such as are godly, be unequally yoked, by marrying with such as are wicked in their life, or maintain damnable heresy [g].

[e] Hebrews 13:4; 1 Timothy 4:3 [f] 1 Corinthians 7:39
[g] Nehemiah 13:25–27

26:4 Marriage ought not to be within the degrees of consanguinity or affinity, forbidden in the Word; [h] nor can such incestuous marriages ever be made lawful, by any law of man or consent of parties, so as those persons may live together as man and wife [i].

[h] Leviticus 18 [i] Mark 6:18; 1 Corinthians 5:1

XXVII. Of the Church

27:1 The catholic or universal church, which (with respect to the internal work of the Spirit and truth of grace) may be called invisible, consists of the whole number of the elect, that have been, are, or shall be gathered into one, under Christ, the head thereof; and is the spouse, the body, the fullness of him that fills all in all [a].

[a] Hebrews 12:23; Colossians 1:18; Ephesians 1:10,22,23;
5:23,27,32

27:2 All persons throughout the world, professing the faith of the gospel, and obedience unto God by Christ according unto it, not destroying their own profession by any errors everting the foundation, or unholiness of conversation, are and may be called visible saints; [b] and of such ought all particular congregations to be constituted [c].

[b] 1 Corinthians 1:2; Acts 11:26 [c] Romans 1:7; Ephesians 1:20–22

27:3 The purest churches under heaven are subject to mixture and error; [d] and some have so degenerated as to become no churches of Christ, but synagogues of Satan; [e] nevertheless Christ always has had, and ever shall have a kingdom in this world, to the end thereof, of such as believe in Him, and make profession of His name [f].

[d] 1 Corinthians 5; Revelation 2,3 [e] Revelation 18:2; 2 Thessalonians 2:11,12 [f] Matthew 16:18; Psalm 72:17, 102:28; Revelation 12:17

27:4 The Lord Jesus Christ is the Head of the church, in whom, by the appointment of the Father, all power for the calling, institution, order or government of the church, is invested in a supreme and sovereign manner; [g] neither can the Pope of Rome in any sense be head thereof, but is that antichrist, that man of sin, and son of perdition, that exalts himself in the church against Christ, and all that is called God; whom the Lord shall destroy with the brightness of His coming [h].

[g] Colossians 1:18; Matthew 28:18–20; Ephesians 4:11,12
[h] 2 Thessalonians 2:2–9

27:5 In the execution of this power wherewith he is so intrusted, the Lord Jesus calls out of the world unto Himself, through the

ministry of His Word, by His Spirit, those that are given unto
Him by His Father, [i] that they may walk before Him in all the
ways of obedience, which He prescribes to them in His Word
[k]. Those thus called, He commands to walk together in particular societies, or churches, for their mutual edification, and
the due performance of that public worship, which He requires
of them in the world [l].

[i] John 10:16; John 12:32 [k] Matthew 28:20 [l] Matthew
18:15–20

27:6 The members of these churches are saints by calling, vis-
ibly manifesting and evidencing (in and by their profession and
walking) their obedience unto that call of Christ; [m] and do
willingly consent to walk together, according to the appointment of Christ; giving up themselves to the Lord, and one to
another, by the will of God, in professed subjection to the ordinances of the Gospel [n].

[m] Romans 1:7; 1 Corinthians 1:2 [n] Acts 2:41,42, 5:13,14;
2 Corinthians 9:13

27:7 To each of these churches thus gathered, according to His
mind declared in His Word, He has given all that power and
authority, which is in any way needful for their carrying on that
order in worship and discipline, which He has instituted for
them to observe; with commands and rules for the due and right
exerting, and executing of that power [o].

[o] Matthew 18:17,18; 1 Corinthians 5:4, 5, 5:13, 2 Corinthians
2:6–8

27:8 A particular church, gathered and completely organized according to the mind of Christ, consists of officers and members; and the officers appointed by Christ to be chosen and set apart by the church (so called and gathered), for the peculiar administration of ordinances, and execution of power or duty, which he entrusts them with, or calls them to, to be continued to the end of the world, are bishops or elders, and deacons [p].

[p] Acts 20:17, 28; Philippians 1:1

27:9 The way appointed by Christ for the calling of any person, fitted and gifted by the Holy Spirit, unto the office of bishop or elder in a church, is, that he be chosen thereunto by the common suffrage of the church itself; [q] and solemnly set apart by fasting and prayer, with imposition of hands of the eldership of the church, if there be any before constituted therein; [r] and of a deacon that he be chosen by the like suffrage, and set apart by prayer, and the like imposition of hands [s].

[q] Acts 14:23 [r] 1 Timothy 4:14 [s] Acts 6:3,5,6

27:10 The work of pastors being constantly to attend the service of Christ, in His churches, in the ministry of the word and prayer, with watching for their souls, as they that must give an account to Him; [t] it is incumbent on the churches to whom they minister, not only to give them all due respect, but also to communicate to them of all their good things according to their ability, [u] so as they may have a comfortable supply, without being themselves entangled in secular affairs; [x] and may also be capable of exercising hospitality towards others; [y] and this is required by the law of nature, and by the express order of our

Lord Jesus, who has ordained that they that preach the Gospel should live of the Gospel [z].

[t] Acts 6:4; Hebrews 13:17 [u] 1 Timothy 5:17,18; Galatians 6:6,7
[x] 2 Timothy 2:4 [y] 1 Timothy 3:2 [z] 1 Corinthians 9:6–14

27:11 Although it be incumbent on the bishops or pastors of the churches, to be instant in preaching the Word, by way of office, yet the work of preaching the word is not so peculiarly confined to them but that others also gifted and fitted by the Holy Spirit for it, and approved and called by the church, may and ought to perform it [a].

[a] Acts 11:19–21; 1 Peter 4:10,11

27:12 As all believers are bound to join themselves to particular churches, when and where they have opportunity so to do; so all that are admitted unto the privileges of a church, are also under the censures and government thereof, according to the rule of Christ [b].

[b] 1 Thessalonians 5:14; 2 Thessalonians 3:6,14,15

27:13 No church members, upon any offense taken by them, having performed their duty required of them towards the person they are offended at, ought to disturb any church-order, or absent themselves from the assemblies of the church, or administration of any ordinances, upon the account of such offense at any of their fellow members, but to wait upon Christ, in the further proceeding of the church [c].

[c] Matthew 18:15–17; Ephesians 4:2,3

27:14. As each church, and all the members of it, are bound to pray continually for the good and prosperity of all the churches of Christ, [d] in all places, and upon all occasions to further every one within the bounds of their places and callings, in the exercise of their gifts and graces, so the churches, when planted by the providence of God, so as they may enjoy opportunity and advantage for it, ought to hold communion among themselves, for their peace, increase of love, and mutual edification [e].

[d] Ephesians 6:18; Psalm 122:6 [e] Romans 16:1,2; 3 John 8–10

27:15 In cases of difficulties or differences, either in point of doctrine or administration, wherein either the churches in general are concerned, or any one church, in their peace, union, and edification; or any member or members of any church are injured, in or by any proceedings in censures not agreeable to truth and order: it is according to the mind of Christ, that many churches holding communion together, do, by their messengers, meet to consider, and give their advice in or about that matter in difference, to be reported to all the churches concerned; [f] howbeit these messengers assembled, are not entrusted with any church-power properly so called; or with any jurisdiction over the churches themselves, to exercise any censures either over any churches or persons; or to impose their determination on the churches or officers [g].

[f] Acts 15:2,4,6,22,23,25 [g] 2 Corinthians 1:24; 1 John 4:1

XXVIII. Of the Communion of Saints

28:1 All saints that are united to Jesus Christ, their head, by His Spirit, and faith, although they are not made thereby one person with Him, have fellowship in His graces, sufferings, death, resurrection, and glory; [a] and, being united to one another in love, they have communion in each others gifts and graces, [b] and are obliged to the performance of such duties, public and private, in an orderly way, as do conduce to their mutual good, both in the inward and outward man [c].

[a] 1 John 1:3; John 1:16; Philippians 3:10; Romans 6:5,6
[b] Ephesians 4:15,16; 1 Corinthians 12:7; 3:21–23 [c] 1 Thessalonians 5:11,14; Romans 1:12; 1 John 3:17,18; Galatians 6:10

28:2 Saints by profession are bound to maintain a holy fellowship and communion in the worship of God, and in performing such other spiritual services as tend to their mutual edification; [d] as also in relieving each other in outward things according to their several abilities, and necessities; [e] which communion, according to the rule of the gospel, though especially to be exercised by them, in the relation wherein they stand, whether in families, [f] or churches, [g] yet, as God offers opportunity, is to be extended to all the household of faith, even all those who in every place call upon the name of the Lord Jesus; nevertheless their communion one with another as saints, does not take away or infringe the title or propriety which each man has in his goods and possessions [h].

[d] Hebrews 10:24,25, 3:12,13 [e] Acts 11:29,30 [f] Ephesians 6:4
[g] 1 Corinthians 12:14–27 [h] Acts 5:4; Ephesians 4:28

XXIX. Of Baptism and the Lord's Supper

29:1 Baptism and the Lord's Supper are ordinances of positive and sovereign institution, appointed by the Lord Jesus, the only lawgiver, to be continued in His church to the end of the world [a].

[a] Matthew 28:19,20; 1 Corinthians 11:26

29:2 These holy appointments are to be administered by those only who are qualified and thereunto called, according to the commission of Christ [b].

[b] Matthew 28:19; 1 Corinthians 4:1

XXX. Of Baptism

30:1 Baptism is an ordinance of the New Testament, ordained by Jesus Christ, to be unto the party baptized, a sign of His fellowship with him, in His death and resurrection; of his being engrafted into Him; [a] of remission of sins; [b] and of his giving up unto God, through Jesus Christ, to live and walk in newness of life [c].

[a] Romans 6:3–5; Colossians 2:12; Galatians 3:27 [b] Mark 1:4; Acts 22:16 [c] Romans 6:4

30:2 Those who do actually profess repentance towards God, faith in, and obedience to, our Lord Jesus Christ, are the only proper subjects of this ordinance [d].

[d] Mark 16:16; Acts 8:36,37, 2:41, 8:12, 18:8

30:3 The outward element to be used in this ordinance is water, wherein the party is to be baptized, in the name of the Father, and of the Son, and of the Holy Spirit [e].

[e] Matthew 28:19,20; Acts 8:38

30:4 Immersion, or dipping of the person in water, is necessary to the due administration of this ordinance [f].

[f] Matthew 3:16; John 3:23

XXXI. Of the Lord's Supper

31:1 The supper of the Lord Jesus was instituted by Him the same night wherein He was betrayed, to be observed in His churches, unto the end of the world, for the perpetual remembrance, and showing to all the world the sacrifice of Himself in His death, [a] confirmation of the faith of believers in all the benefits thereof, their spiritual nourishment, and growth in him, their further engagement in, and to all duties which they owe to him; and to be a bond and pledge of their communion with Him, and with each other [b].

[a] 1 Corinthians 11:23–26 [b] 1 Corinthians 10:16,17,21

31:2 In this ordinance Christ is not offered up to His Father, nor any real sacrifice made at all for remission of sin of the quick or dead, but only a memorial of that one offering up of Himself by Himself upon the cross, once for all; [c] and a spiritual oblation of all possible praise unto God for the same [d]. So that the popish sacrifice of the mass, as they call it, is most abominable, injurious to Christ's own only sacrifice the alone propitiation for all the sins of the elect.

[c] Hebrews 9:25,26,28 [d] 1 Corinthians 11:24; Matthew 26:26,27

31:3 The Lord Jesus has, in this ordinance, appointed His ministers to pray, and bless the elements of bread and wine, and thereby to set them apart from a common to a holy use, and to take and break the bread; to take the cup, and, they communicating also themselves, to give both to the communicants [e].

[e] 1 Corinthians 11:23–26, etc.

31:4 The denial of the cup to the people, worshipping the elements, the lifting them up, or carrying them about for adoration, and reserving them for any pretended religious use, are all contrary to the nature of this ordinance, and to the institution of Christ [f].

[f] Matthew 26:26–28, 15:9, Exodus 20:4,5

31:5 The outward elements in this ordinance, duly set apart to the uses ordained by Christ, have such relation to him crucified, as that truly, although in terms used figuratively, they are sometimes called by the names of the things they represent, to wit, the body and blood of Christ, [g] albeit, in substance and nature, they still remain truly and only bread and wine, as they were before [h].

[g] 1 Corinthians 11:27 [h] 1 Corinthians 11:26–28

31:6 That doctrine which maintains a change of the substance of bread and wine, into the substance of Christ's body and blood, commonly called transubstantiation, by consecration of a priest, or by any other way, is repugnant not to Scripture alone, [i] but even to common sense and reason, overthrows the nature of the ordinance, and has been, and is, the cause of manifold superstitions, yea, of gross idolatries [k].

[i] Acts 3:21; Luke 14:6,39 [k] 1 Corinthians 11:24,25

31:7 Worthy receivers, outwardly partaking of the visible elements in this ordinance, do then also inwardly by faith, really and indeed, yet not carnally and corporally, but spiritually receive, and feed upon Christ crucified, and all the benefits of His death; the body and blood of Christ being then not corporally or carnally, but spiritually present to the faith of believers in that ordinance, as the elements themselves are to their outward senses [l].

[l] 1 Corinthians 10:16, 11:23–26

31:8 All ignorant and ungodly persons, as they are unfit to enjoy communion with Christ, so are they unworthy of the Lord's table, and cannot, without great sin against Him, while they remain such, partake of these holy mysteries, or be admitted thereunto; [m] yea, whosoever shall receive unworthily, are guilty of the body and blood of the Lord, eating and drinking judgment to themselves [n].

[m] 2 Corinthians 6:14,15 [n] 1 Corinthians 11:29; Matthew 7:6

XXXII. Of the State of Man after Death, And of the Resurrection of the Dead

32:1 The bodies of men after death return to dust, and see corruption; [a] but their souls, which neither die nor sleep, having an immortal subsistence, immediately return to God who gave them [b]. The souls of the righteous being then made perfect in holiness, are received into paradise, where they are with Christ, and behold the face of God in light and glory, waiting for the full redemption of their bodies; [c] and the souls of the wicked are cast into hell; where they remain in torment and utter darkness, reserved to the judgment of the great day; [d] besides these two places, for souls separated from their bodies, the Scripture acknowledges none.

[a] Genesis 3:19; Acts 13:36 [b] Ecclesiastes 12:7 [c] Luke 23:43; 2 Corinthians 5:1,6,8; Phil. 1:23; Hebrews 12:23 [d] Jude 6,7; 1 Peter 3:19; Luke 16:23,24

32:2 At the last day, such of the saints as are found alive, shall not sleep, but be changed; [e] and all the dead shall be raised up with the selfsame bodies, and none other; [f] although with different qualities, which shall be united again to their souls forever [g].

[e] 1 Corinthians 15:51,52; 1 Thessalonians 4:17 [f] Job 19:26,27 [g] 1 Corinthians 15:42,43

32:3 The bodies of the unjust shall, by the power of Christ, be raised to dishonor; the bodies of the just, by His Spirit, unto honor, and be made conformable to His own glorious body [h].

[h] Acts 24:15; John 5:28,29; Philippians 3:21

XXXIII. Of the Last Judgment

33:1 God has appointed a day wherein he will judge the world in righteousness, by Jesus Christ; [a] to whom all power and judgment is given of the Father; in which day, not only the apostate angels shall be judged, [b] but likewise all persons that have lived upon the earth shall appear before the tribunal of Christ, to give an account of their thoughts, words, and deeds, and to receive according to what they have done in the body, whether good or evil [c].

[a] Acts 17:31; John 5:22,27 [b] 1 Corinthians 6:3; Jude 6
[c] 2 Corinthians 5:10; Ecclesiastes 12:14; Matthew 12:36;
Romans 14:10,12; Matthew 25:32–46

33:2 The end of God's appointing this day, is for the manifestation of the glory of His mercy, in the eternal salvation of the elect; and of His justice, in the eternal damnation of the reprobate, who are wicked and disobedient; [d] for then shall the righteous go into everlasting life, and receive that fullness of joy and glory with everlasting rewards, in the presence of the Lord; but the wicked, who do not know God, and do not obey the gospel of Jesus Christ, shall be cast aside into everlasting torments, [e] and punished with everlasting destruction, from the presence of the Lord, and from the glory of His power [f].

[d] Romans 9:22,23 [e] Matthew 25:21,34; 2 Timothy 4:8
[f] Matthew 25:46; Mark 9:48; 2 Thessalonians 1:7–10

33:3 As Christ would have us to be certainly persuaded that there shall be a day of judgment, both to deter all men from sin, [g] and for the greater consolation of the godly in their adversity, [h] so will he have the day unknown to men, that they may shake off all carnal security, and be always watchful, because they know not at what hour the Lord will come, [i] and may ever be prepared to say, *Come Lord Jesus; come quickly* [k]. Amen.

[g] 2 Corinthians 5:10,11 [h] 2 Thessalonians 1:5–7 [i] Mark 13:35–37; Luke 12:35–40 [k] Revelation 22:20

APPENDIX 2: A SUMMARY OF CHURCH DISCIPLINE

A Summary of Church Discipline Showing the Qualifications and Duties of the Officers and Members of a Gospel Church

By The Baptist Association
in Charleston, South Carolina

For this Cause left I thee in Crete, that thou shouldest set in Order the Things that are wanting (Titus 1:5).

See that thou makest all things according to the Pattern shewed to thee in the Mount (Hebrews 8:5).

CHARLESTON
PRINTED BY DAVID BRUCE
MDCCLXXIV

PREFACE

THE following *Summary of Church Discipline*, being designed chiefly for the benefit of the poor and unlearned, is contracted into a very narrow compass, and exhibited in the plainest language. This, with whatever defects it has, will require the candor of the more learned and intelligent.

To remove, in some measure, the ignorance of but too many church members, about discipline, was the principal motive for engaging in this work.

We mean not to impose our sentiments on any person whatever, or to anathematize those who differ from us in opinion. The Word of God and no human composition, is the standard, by which our principles and conduct must be tried.

Nevertheless, we hope this small piece may be of some use, for the right understanding of God's Word, with regard to the points treated on; and we desire that the Scriptures referred to may be carefully consulted, to see whether these things be true.

Some may say, "There is no call for this publication, seeing there is such a valuable treatise on church-discipline, published some years ago by the Philadelphia Association."

We mean not to depreciate the value of that piece; it has merited much from the Baptist Churches; but it is out of print, and we apprehend not so explicit as this; besides some things therein appear to us exceptionable. However, we have borrowed many hints from it; and are greatly indebted to the late learned, pious and judicious Dr. Gill, for what is taken from his *Exposition and Body of Divinity*.

May the Great Head of the Church bless this feeble attempt to promote His honor, and the welfare of His churches.

I. Of a True and Orderly Gospel Church

1. GOD in every age has had, has, and will have a church or people in the world, consisting of a greater or less number, and subsisting under various forms and in diverse circumstances (Acts 7:38, Ephesians 3:21).

The catholic or universal church, considered collectively forms one complete and glorious body (Song of Solomon 6:9) called Christ's mystical body, of which He is the head (Colossians 1:18, Ephesians 1:22). This is the general assembly and church of the first born, which are written in heaven (Hebrews 12:23).

Under the Old Testament dispensation, the church was pretty much confined to family or nation; but under the present administration Christ gathers to Himself a people from among all nations (Matthew 28:19, 20). And being thus gathered, by the power of Christ in the gospel, it becomes their duty to unite in distinct churches (Acts 2:41, 47), that they may walk together, *in all the commandments and ordinances of the Lord blameless*. Hence we find that under the gospel, churches were settled wherever there was a sufficient number of converts for that purpose (Revelation 2 and 3).

A particular gospel church consists of a company of saints incorporated by a special covenant into one distinct body, and meeting together in one place, for the enjoyment of fellowship with each other and with Christ their head, in all His institutions, to their mutual edification and the glory of God through the Spirit (2 Corinthians 8:5, Acts 2:1).

2. The temple of the Lord is not to be built with dead but living materials (1 Peter 2:5). None have a right to church mem-

bership but such as Christ will own as His sincere followers at the last decisive day, whatever pretensions they may make to an interest in His favor (Matthew 7:22, 23). Except a man be born again, he has no right to enter into the kingdom of God, or into a gospel church (John 3:3). Christ is a living Head and will have none but living members in His mystical body (John 15:6).

3. The constitution of churches is plainly supposed (Acts 2:47, Matthew 18:17, etc.) and it is necessary, in order that the disciples of Christ may enjoy the ordinance of the Lord's Supper, which is a church ordinance, that they watch over one another, warn the unruly, and lay censures on disorderly and impenitent persons.

The Scriptures do not absolutely determine the number of persons necessary to constitute a church; but as our Lord has said, *Where two or three are gathered together in My name, there am I in the midst of them* (Matthew 18:20), it should seem as if that number of godly persons might, at least in some urgent cases, form a church essential, though not a church complete, or duly organized, for lack of officers. Experience has sometimes proved that such small beginnings have been succeeded with a large increase, consistent with that encouraging promise (Isaiah 60:22), *a little one shall become a thousand, and a small one a strong nation*.

A gospel church is not national, but congregational. This was evidently the case in the apostolic age; hence Paul sent a general epistle to the several churches in Galatia (Galatians 1:1, 2) and our Lord Himself ordered epistles to be written to the seven distinct churches in Asia (Revelation 2 and 3).

With regard to the manner of constituting a church, it must be by the consent and desire of the parties concerned; and it will be expedient to call in a minister or ministers, if to be had, to assist on that important occasion. The parties being met fasting, the solemnity ought to be opened by fervent prayer to God (Philippians 4:6); next a sermon suitable to the occasion should be preached; and then, for the mutual satisfaction of every individual, a strict inquiry should be made into their experience of a work of grace on their hearts, their soundness in the doctrines of faith and the goodness of their lives and conversation; unless, as members of churches, they come honorably recommended for that purpose. Being thus satisfied with each other's graces and qualifications, and united in the bond of love they should give up themselves to the Lord and to one another by the will of God (2 Corinthians 8:5) by subscribing a written covenant consistent with the Word of God (Isaiah 44:5), thereby binding and obliging themselves to be the Lord's, to walk in all His commands and ordinances, and in all respects to behave towards each other as brethren, agreeable to the spiritual relation they now enter into.

Being thus united in one body, under Christ their head, they become and are to be deemed a church essential, founded on the gospel plan. Let them then ratify their engagements by a participation of the Lord's supper, and so conclude the solemnity.

4. A church thus constituted has the keys, or power of government, within itself, having Christ for its head, and His law for its rule. It has the power and privilege of choosing its own officers (Acts 6:3, 13:2), exercising its own discipline (Matthew 18:17) and of administering the Word and ordinances, for the edification and comfort of its members (Acts 2:46). All which, with every other act of discipline, each distinct church may exercise, without being subject to the cognizance of any other church, presbytery, synod, or council whatever (1 Corinthians 5:12, Matthew 18:17).

Churches being vested with such power ought to use it with prudence lest they dishonor Christ and His cause or wound their fellow members (1 Corinthians 10:31, Rom. 15:2). To guard against which, church business should be debated deliberately with humility and moderation; that, if possible, the members may be unanimous in all their determinations. Nevertheless, when this unanimity cannot be attained, a majority of the male members may determine, and the minority ought peaceably to submit. This appears not only from that general rule (Ephesians 5:21), *submitting yourselves one to another in the fear of God*; but more clearly from 2 Corinthians 2:6, *sufficient to such a man is this punishment, which was inflicted of many*: Which *many* supposes a majority; in the original it is *hupo ton pleionon, by the more*, the greater or major part. Which plainly points out a decision by a majority.

Female members may, when called upon, act as witnesses in a church; and when aggrieved, are to make known their case, either in person or by a brother; and must have a proper regard paid them. But they are excluded from all share of rule or government in the church (1 Corinthians 14:34, 35; 1 Timothy 2:11, 12).

II. Of Church Officers

THE ordinary officers of the church, and the only ones now existing, are ministers and deacons (Philippians 1:1). In the first gospel churches there were other officers such as apostles, prophets, and evangelists (1 Corinthians 12:28, Ephesians 4:11), who were endowed with extraordinary gifts, which were then necessary for the confirmation of the gospel, but have since become extinct.

1. Ministers of the gospel, who are frequently called elders, bishops, pastors and teachers, are appointed by Christ to the highest office in the church, and therefore need peculiar qualifications such as are pointed out (1 Timothy 3:2–7 and Titus 1:5–10).

As they have the charge of souls, and are leaders in the house of God, churches cannot be too careful in choosing men to the ministerial function. They ought to be men fearing God, being born again of the Spirit, sound in the faith, and of blameless lives and conversations, as becomes the gospel of Christ, having fervent desires to glorify God and save souls (John 3:10, 2 Timothy 1:13, 1 Timothy 3:2, Romans 9:3, 10:1).

A church having no minister should look among its own members and see if there be any who seem to have promising gifts and graces for that great work. If such a one is found, he is to be put on private trial for a season; when on finding him promising, and that they are edified by his preaching, they may call him to preach in public. After which, if it should appear that his rod, like Aaron's, buds, blossoms, and bears fruit, he is to be set apart by ordination, that he may perform every part of the sacred function (Acts 13:2, 3). But should no such person be found in the church, it is the duty of a sister church, if possible, to supply them. And if a person, who is a member of another church be approved, and be inclined to accept a call from them, he must first become a member with them, so that they may choose him from among themselves (see Acts 1:21). Thus were deacons chosen (Acts 6:3).

The candidate having accepted the call of the church, they proceed to his ordination, which is to be done in the following manner, viz. If there is not a sufficient presbytery in the church, neighboring elders are to be called and authorized to perform that service. The day is set apart by fasting and prayer (Acts 13:2, 3; 14:23). The elders [ministers] being satisfied with regard to the gifts, graces, soundness of principles, and becoming life and conversation of the candidate; the church being met, and giving their suffrage for his ordination, a sermon is to be preached on the occasion, and he declaring his willingness and inward call to take upon him the sacred office (1 Corinthians 9:16). A public confession of his faith will be required, then the ministers lay their hands on his head and by prayer set him apart to the great work of the ministry. This done, they give him the right hand of fellowship (Galatians 2:9), and then one of the ministers publicly gives him a charge or directory how to behave himself in the house of God (2 Timothy 4:5). The solemnity is concluded by prayer, singing, and a blessing on the whole congregation.

A minister, being ordained, has authority from Christ to preach the gospel and baptize believers in any part of the world where God, in His providence, may call him. But if he should be called unto and accept the pastoral charge of any particular church, he will be more immediately confined to them and they to him (1 Peter 5:1–3).

Persons thus commissioned are to attend to their work with all possible engagedness, as it becomes those who have the charge of souls. They must give themselves up to study, prayer, and meditation (1 Timothy 4:14–16), that they may be workmen who need not be ashamed (2 Timothy 2:15). They must be instant in season and out of season, preaching the pure doctrines of the gospel (2 Timothy 1:13; 4:2). They are to feed the Lord's flock with spiritual bread (Acts 20:28), to preach with the view of bringing souls to Christ, and not for the sake of honor or *filthy lucre*. They are not to lord it over God's heritage, but to be patient and tenderhearted (1 Peter 5:3; 2 Timothy 2:24, 25). They are to watch over the flock, *to comfort the feebleminded* (1 Thessalonians 5:14); to sound the alarm to the wicked and obstinate (Ezekiel 3:17, 18); and to set their faces like flints against profaneness and every vice.

They should often visit the flock committed to their charge, to know the state of their souls, that they may speak a word in season to them, catechize the youth, instruct the ignorant, and pray with and for them. They are especially to visit the sick and those who are otherwise afflicted (Ezekiel 34:4).

They are to administer the ordinances of the gospel in a strict conformity to the Word of God (Hebrews 8:5), to preside in the affairs of the church, and see that strict discipline is duly executed therein (Hebrews 13:7, 17). In a word, they are to be examples to the flock, *in word, in conversation, in charity, in spirit, in faith, and in purity* (1 Timothy 4:12).

2. As it is the duty of ministers more particularly to give themselves to prayer and to the ministry of the Word, God has appointed officers to be employed in the inferior services of the church, namely deacons, whose qualifications are pointed out (Acts 6:3, 1 Tim. 3:8-13).

Deacons are likewise to be chosen by the suffrage of the church from among its own members, and, being first proved, are to be set apart to that office by prayer and laying on of hands (Acts 6:2–6).

The office of a deacon is to relieve the minister from the secular concerns of the church; hence they are called Helps (1 Corinthians 12:28). Their business is to serve tables; "The table of the Lord, by providing the bread and wine for it; receiving both from the minister, when blessed, and distributing them to the members; and collecting from them for the poor, and the defraying the charge; and observing what members are missing at the ordinance, whom they are to admonish; and if their admonitions are not regarded, to report it to the church: and they are likewise to serve the minister's table, by taking care that he has a sufficient competency for his support; and it belongs to them to stir up the members of the church to their duty in communicating to him; and what they receive of them, they are to apply to his use: and also, they are to serve the poor's table; to whom they are to distribute of the church's stock, with all impartiality, simplicity, cheerfulness and sympathy" (Dr. Gill on Acts 6:2). By the faithful discharge of their office, they shall *purchase to themselves a good degree, and great boldness in the faith* (1 Timothy 3:13).

III. Of Receiving Persons to Church Membership

A CHURCH thus founded on the Scripture plan ought to observe good order, as in all other cases, so also in the admission of members into their community.

1. Every well regulated society requires qualifications in its members; much more should a church of Jesus Christ be careful that none be admitted into its communion, but such as are possessed of those prerequisites pointed out in Scripture.

They must be truly gracious persons. None are fit materials of a gospel church, without having first experienced an entire change of nature (Matthew 18:3), *Verily I say unto you, except ye be converted, and become as little children, ye shall not enter into the kingdom of heaven.* By which is intended a *gospel church state*, as the context clearly shows. To the same purpose is John 3:5. Christ's church is a spiritual house, built up of lively stones, i.e. of *living souls* (1 Peter 2:5). By nature we are dead in trespasses and sins, and Christ does not place such dead materials in His spiritual building. It is certain the Ephesian church was not composed of such materials (Ephesians 2:1). The members of the church at Rome were the *called of Jesus Christ* (Romans 1:6), *called out of darkness into the Lord's marvelous light* (1 Peter 2:9), *called to be saints* (Romans 1:7), as were the members of the church at Corinth (1 Corinthians 1:2), and the churches in general are called *churches of the saints* (1 Corinthians 14:33). The members of the church at Colosse are denominated not only *saints*, but *faithful brethren in Christ* (Colossians 1:2), or true believers in Him. None but such have a right to ordinances (Acts 8:37). Without faith none discern the Lord's body in the Supper, and consequently must eat and drink unworthily (1 Corinthians 11:29). Indeed *without faith it is impossible to please God* (Hebrews 11:6).

The Church of England, in her Articles, defines a gospel church as "a congregation of faithful men, in which the pure word of God is preached, and the sacraments duly administered." Of such "faithful men" or believers in Christ was the first church at Jerusalem composed (Acts 2:41; 5:14). Those whom *the Lord add to the church* were *such as should be saved* (Acts 2:47). Let those look to it who make the church of Christ a harlot by opening the door of admission so wide as to suffer unbelievers, unconverted, and graceless persons to crowd into it without control.

They should be persons of some competent knowledge of divine and spiritual things; who have not only knowledge of themselves, and of their lost state by nature, and of the way of salvation by Christ; but have some degree of knowledge of God in his nature, perfections, and works; and of Christ in His person as the Son of God, of His proper deity, of His incarnation, of His offices as prophet, priest, and king; of justification by His righteousness, pardon by His blood, satisfaction by His sacrifice, and of His prevalent intercession. And also of the Spirit of God: His person, offices and operations; and of the important truths of the gospel, and doctrines of grace; or how otherwise should the church be *the pillar and ground of truth?*

Their lives and conversations ought to be such as *becometh the gospel of Christ* (Philippians 1:27); that is holy, just, and upright (Psalm 15:1, 2); if their practice contradicts their profession they are not to be admitted to church membership. Holiness becomes the Lord's house forever (Psalm 93:5).

They ought to be truly baptized in water, i.e., by immersion, upon a profession of their faith, agreeable to the ancient practice of John the Baptist and the apostles of our Lord Jesus Christ (Matthew 3:6, John 3:23, Romans 6:4 , Acts 8:36–38). It is allowed by all that baptism is essential to church communion and ought to precede it; there is not one instance in the Word of God of any being admitted without it; the three thousand penitents, after they had *gladly received* the Word, *were baptized*; and then, and not before, were added to the church; so the first church at Samaria consisted of men and women baptized by Philip, they believing what he said concerning the kingdom of God. And Lydia and her household, and the jailor and his, being baptized upon their faith, laid the foundation of the church at Philippi. And the church at Corinth was begun with persons who hearing the Word, believed and were baptized; and the church at Ephesus was first formed by some disciples baptized in the name of the Lord Jesus (Acts 2:41; 8:12; 16:15, 31–33; 18:8; 19:5). So the members of the churches at Rome, Galatia, and Colosse were baptized persons (Romans 6:3, 4; Galatians 3:27; Colossians 2:12).

2. Persons making application are to be admitted into the communion of a church by the common suffrage of its members; being first satisfied that they have the qualifications laid down in the preceding section; for which purpose candidates must come under examination before the church; and if it should happen that they do not give satisfaction, they should be set aside until a more satisfactory profession is made (1 Timothy 6:12).

It may be that one or two of the members of the church have conceived a prejudice against a person applying for fellowship; in this case they are to be duly heard and if their objections are of sufficient weight the candidate must be set aside; if not, the majority of voices ought, in all reason, to decide it. When the church concludes that the person applying for membership may be admitted the minister is to acquaint him with the rules and orders of God's house; and upon his promising, covenanting, and agreeing strictly to observe them, as assisted by the Spirit of God, the minister, in behalf of the church, is to give him the right hand of fellowship, and to receive him as a member into union and full communion with that particular church; whereby he becomes entitled to all the rights and privileges thereof (Colossians 2:19, Romans 15:7, 2 Corinthians 8:5).

If a member should desire a transient or occasional communion in any church to which he does not belong, if it be well known that he is an orderly person, he may be admitted to the Lord's table; but he should have nothing to do with the government of the church, unless his advice and assistance be asked. But a person unknown should by no means be admitted without a satisfactory letter of recommendation from the church to which he belongs.

When a member removes his residence nearer to another church of the same faith and order, he is bound in duty to procure a letter of dismission from the church to which he belongs (Acts 18:27). And the church to which he is removed is bound in duty to receive him into union and full communion, unless it should appear that he is either immoral in his life or unsound in his principles. But let it be remembered that he continues a member of his own church from whence he came until he is received into the church to which he is removing (Acts 9:26–28). That it is the duty of a believer to give himself as a member of an orderly church nearest to his place of residence, or which he can most conveniently attend, appears plain from the following considerations: (1) by the neglect of this duty he will deprive himself of the edification, comfort, loving instruction, watchful care, and faithful admonitions of his fellow members; (2) it would give room to suspect he was impatient of that restraint which every humble member deems his mercy; (3) it would seem as if he aimed at screening himself from necessary contributions, or church discipline; (4) such a neglect casts a manifest contempt on the church and ministry near which he resides; (5) were this conduct to be allowed and become general, it would cause great confusion among the churches; and as such a practice can suit none but careless and disorderly persons, the church they belong to ought to admonish them and if they still persist, to censure them.

The same reasons hold good against those who require a dismission from the church they belong to unto one more remote. If one member may be so dismissed, another may, even officers of the church as well as others. To dismiss a member to the world at large, would be yet more preposterous, and ought never to be done in any other way than by excommunication. The usual plea for such an unreasonable request is either that they cannot profit under such a ministry or that the concerns of the church are not properly managed; but the truth is pride is generally at the bottom of such desires, for an humble Christian will esteem others better than himself, bear with the infirmities of the weak, and pray and hope to find a blessing where Providence casts his lot.

It sometimes happens that an orderly member is called by Providence to remove, but (like Abraham, Hebrews 11:8) he knows not whither; in such case the church to which he belongs ought to furnish him with a letter of commendation, permitting him to join any church of the same faith and order, where Providence may cast his lot (Colossians 4:10). On his being admitted into any such church, he is dismissed from the church of which he was a member, and notice thereof should be given them as soon as possible.

Members who have been suspended or excommunicated by the church and giving satisfactory evidence of their repentance are to be cautioned against the evils of which they were guilty; and on their promising, with the Lord's assistance, to lead orderly lives for the future, they are to be again received into full communion with the church and have the right hand of fellowship given them (Galatians 6:1, 2; 2 Corinthians 2:7, 8), but they are not on any account to be rebaptized (Ephesians 4:5).

IV. Of the Duties Incumbent on Church Members

A CHURCH constituted after the heavenly pattern is as a city set on a hill, from which the glories of rich and free grace abundantly shine (Psalm 50:2). The true members of it have the light of the gospel shining in their hearts, by the Holy Spirit, and are entitled to all the blessings of the new covenant (Ephesians 1:3). And being thus blessed, their faith is a lively, active faith, not only purifying their hearts, but working by love (Galatians 5:6), whereby they become the light of the world (Matthew 5:14–16), which they make apparent by a faithful discharge of the duties enjoined them by the Lord Jesus Christ, the great Head of the church (James 2:18).

1. As ministers are the representatives of Christ, and employed by Him in a work that is both useful and honorable, there are certain duties incumbent on all members of churches toward them. As (1) they owe them distinguishing honor and reverence, and are to hold them in reputation as the ambassadors of Christ (Philippians 2:29; 2 Corinthians 5:20), and to esteem them highly for their work's sake (1 Thessalonians 5:13). (2) They are to contribute, according to their respective abilities, towards their ministers support (Galatians 6:6), that, being freed as much as possible from the cares of life, they may wholly devote themselves to the duties of their holy function, and have it in their power to use hospitality (1 Timothy 3:2), and stretch out the benevolent hand of charity to the poor in distress (Galatians 2:10), which maintenance ought not to be considered as a gratuity, but as a debt due to their minister. The law of nature requires it (1 Timothy 5:18). In the Lord's grants to Israel there was always a reserve made for the priests; under the gospel, pro-

vision is made for the support of its ministers (1 Corinthians 9:7–14). (3) They are to obey and submit themselves to their ministers (Ephesians 6:18–20). (4) They ought to stand by and assist them in all their troubles and afflictions (2 Timothy 4:16, Job 6:14). (5) They should receive no accusation against them without full proof (1 Timothy 5:19). (6) Nor should they expose their infirmities (Acts 23:5, 3 John 10). (7) They should follow their example, as far as they follow Christ (2 Thessalonians 3: 7; 1 Corinthians 11:1).

2. Deacons being in an honorable office in the church, the members are: (1) to respect and esteem them as being employed by the Lord to serve in the household of faith, and as men whom (if faithful) God will greatly honor and bless (1 Timothy 3:13, Matthew 25:21); (2) to submit to their godly and friendly admonitions (1 Corinthians 16:16); (3) to encourage them in their office by cheerful and liberal contributions for the service of God's house, his ministers, and his poor (2 Corinthians 9:6, 7).

3. The members of a church are bound in duty (1) to love all men, but especially to love and do good to them who are of the household of faith (Galatians 6:10), all must be done from a principle of love (1 John 4: 7–11, John 13:3 4, 35); (2) to follow after the things which make for peace (Romans 14:19), in order to which they are to put the most favorable construction on words and actions that are doubtful (1 Corinthians 13:7), and to speak no evil one of another (James 4:11), and to endeavor, by a disinterested and godly behavior, to sow the fruit of righteousness in peace (James 3:18), carefully avoiding whisperings and backbitings (2 Corinthians 12:20), not to be busy meddlers wit h the concerns of others (2 Thessalonians 3:11), not to take up an evil report against another (Acts 25:16), nor do any thing through strife and vain glory (Philippians 2:3); (3) to endeavor

after each other's edification and growth in grace (1 Thessalonians 5:11, 2 Pet. 3:18); (4) to pray for each other (James 5:16); (5) to visit each other, especially when sick or otherwise afflicted (Acts 15:36, James 1:27), and those visits ought to be improved for edification, therefore they should spend the time in praying together (Psalm 34:3), in godly conversation (Malachi 3:16), in exhorting and encouraging each other (Hebrews 3:13, Psalm 55:14), warning and admonishing one another (1 Thessalonians 5:14, Romans 15:14), ingenuously confessing their faults to one another, so far as Christian prudence will permit (James 5:16), and administering all possible relief to the needy and distressed (James 2:15, 16); (6) to avoid, as much as possible, going to law with each other (1 Corinthians 6:1–7); (7) to prefer marrying among themselves as far as it may be done with prudence (Amos 3:3, 2 Corinthians 6:14); (8) and to labor to find out the cause of shyness in a brother, as soon as it is discovered (Matthew 5:23, 24).

4. The duties of members to the church are: (1) to pray for its peace and prosperity, and use their utmost endeavors to promote its welfare (Psalm 122:6–9), (2) they ought carefully to attend all church meetings, whether for public worship or business (Hebrews 10:25, Psalm 84:4, 10); (3) it is their duty to submit to the order and discipline of the church, so far as it is consistent with the Word of God (Deuteronomy 5:1, Hebrews 13:17); (4) they are to employ their talents and freely bestow of their substance for the service of the church (Romans 12:6–8, Proverbs 3:9, 10); (5) they must carefully avoid jarrings, contentions and quarrels in the church (1 Corinthians 10:32, Romans 2:8); (6) and they must not divulge any of the church's secrets (Song of Solomon 4:12).

V. Of Church Censures

REWARDS and penalties give sanction to law; therefore our Lord Jesus Christ, who is the only supreme Head of the church, in giving laws and institutions for the government thereof, has annexed rewards of grace to the faithful and obedient observers of them and punishments to be inflicted on the rebellious (Hebrews 11:6, Romans 2:6–9, Revelation 22:12).

There are some punishments which our righteous Lawgiver inflicts more immediately with His own hand, either by His providence in this world or by the execution of divine wrath in the world to come. There are other punishments which Christ, by His Word, authorizes His church to inflict on its rebellious and unworthy members. These are commonly called church censures, which differ in their nature according to the nature and degree of the offense, and may be denominated rebuke, suspension, and excommunication.

1. Rebuke or admonition (the lowest degree of church censure) is a reproving of an offender, pointing out the offense, charging it upon the conscience, advising and exhorting him to repentance, watchfulness, and new obedience, and praying for him that he may be reclaimed (Titus 1:13). This, and all other church censures, must be administered in love and tenderness (Revelation 3:19), with Christian prudence (1 Timothy 1:3), a sincere aim to save the soul from death (James 5:19, 20; 2 Corinthians 13:10; Galatians 6:1), without partiality (1 Timothy 5:21), and for a caution to others (1 Timothy 5:20).

A member becomes worthy of rebuke, (1) when he wounds the conscience of a weak brother, by the use of things in themselves indifferent (1 Corinthians 8:11, 12); (2) when he exposes the infirmities of a brother to others (1 Peter 4:8); (3) when he

disquiets the peace of the brethren about matters of indiffer-
ence (Romans 14:19–22); (4) when he indulges anger against
a brother, without a just cause (Matthew 5:22); (5) when he is
contentious about unscriptural forms and fashions, as if they
were necessary to be used in the church or among the members
(1 Corinthians 11:16); (6) when he neglects privately to admonish or reprove a brother whom he knows to be guilty of sin (Leviticus 19:17); (7) when he neglects to attend church meetings
for business (Acts 6:2); (8) and when he attends other places of
worship to the neglect of his own (Hebrews 10:25).

2. Suspension, considered as a church censure, is that act of
a church whereby an offending member, being found guilty, is
set aside from office, from the Lord's table, and from the liberty
of judging or voting in any case. By this act the staff beauty is
broken, but not the staff bands (Zechariah 11:10, 14). Therefore
as this censure does not cut off from union, but only from communion with the church, the suspended member is not to be ac-
counted as enemy, but admonished as a brother (2 Thessalonians
3:15), and upon a credible profession of repentance the censure
is to be taken off and the delinquent restored to all the privileges
of the church.

This censure is to be administered in case of crimes which
do not amount so high as to deserve excommunication, as (1)
when a member breaks the peace of the church by janglings and
disputings (1 Timothy 1:6; 6:5); (2) when he withdraws from the
church on account of its wholesome discipline, notwithstanding loving admonitions have been given him (John 6:66, Jude
19); (3) when he leaves his place at the Lord's table for the sake
of another member with whom he is offended, and neglects to
do his duty by him as directed (Matthew 18:15); (4) when he
broaches unsound, heretical principles (Titus 3:10); (5) when

he is a busy tattler and backbiter (Psalm 50:19–21); (6) when he through sloth neglects the necessary duties of life (1 Timothy 5:8); (7) when he has committed a gross crime but gives some tokens of repentance, he is to be suspended that the church may have time to judge of his sincerity (1 John 4:1); (8) and when a party of members, like Korah and his company, break through their covenant obligations and attempt to set up for themselves, in an irregular manner and in opposition to all the loving persuasions of the majority, such are *trucebreakers* and *despisers of those that are good* (2 Timothy 3:3). In a word, all practices that in their own nature and tendency are destructive of the reputation, peace, and prosperity of the church and yet appear not to be past remedy, merit this censure.

3. As excommunication is on all hands acknowledged to be an ordinance of Christ, the great Head of the church, and a censure in its own nature, very important, awful, and tremendous, it is highly needful that churches should well understand the nature of it.

Excommunication is a censure of the highest degree; it is a judicial act of the church in which, by the authority of Christ, she cuts off and entirely excludes an unworthy member from union and communion with the church, and from all the rights and privileges thereof. "It is a disfranchising from all the immunities of a fellow-citizen with the saints, and taking from him a place and a name in the house of God" (Gill).

This censure, awful as it is, respects only the spiritual concerns of a man, as related to the church, and does by no means affect his temporal estate, or civil affairs; it does not subject him to fines, imprisonment, or death; it does not interfere with the business of the civil magistrate; nor does it break in upon the natural and civil relations between man and wife, parents and children, masters and servants; nor forbid attendance on the external ministry of the Word.

To deliver an offender *unto Satan for the destruction of the flesh* (1 Corinthians 5:5) was an act purely Apostolical, for it was not the act of the church; "nor is this a form of excommunication; nor was this phrase ever used in excommunicating persons by the primitive churches; nor ought it ever to be used; it is what no man, or set of men, have power to do now, since the ceasing of the extraordinary gifts of the Spirit, which the apostles were endowed with; who, as they had a power over Satan to dispossess him from the bodies of men, so to deliver up the bodies of men into his hands" (Dr. Gill on the text). Hence the apostle writing to Timothy on a similar case, expresses it as done by himself, and not by the church (1 Timothy 1:20).

The act of excommunication is expressed by various phrases; as by avoiding familiar conversation with such (Romans 16:17), by not keeping company with them (1 Corinthians 5:9; Ephesians 5:11), by not eating with them at the Lord's table (1 Corinthians 5:11) by purging out from the church the old leaven (1 Corinthians 5:7), by putting away the wicked from among them (1 Cor. 5:13), by withdrawing from disorderly persons, and by cutting them off from fellowship with the saints (2 Thessalonians 3:6; Galatians 5:12).

The subjects of this ordinance are members who are guilty of notorious and atrocious crimes, which are so, either in their own nature or by means of sundry aggravations. There are some crimes so high and pernicious in their own nature as to call for a speedy excommunication, unless the most evident marks of repentance appear in the offender, as (1) all sins that are against the letter of the ten commandments (Romans 7:12, Matthews 5:17); (2) all that call for severe corporal punishments from human laws, provided those laws are not contrary to the laws of God (Proverbs 8:15, Romans 13:1–4, 1 Peter 2:13, 14); (3) and all such sins as are highly scandalous in their nature and expose the church to contempt (1 Timothy 5:24; 1 Corinthians 5:2). We find black catalogs of sins which call for this censure in 1 Corinthians 5:11 and 6:9–10. And indeed for crimes of an inferior nature, when aggravated by a contumacious [stubbornly rebellious] despising of the authority of the church (after the more gentle censures have been used) excommunication ought to take place.

But an offender, even of the highest rank, who gives clear, evident, and satisfactory proofs of a true, sincere, evangelical repentance is by no means to be excommunicated. Does not reason itself suggest that we ought to forgive those who repent, and those whom God has forgiven? Christ our great pattern did so, as appears in the case of the woman taken in adultery (John 8:11). Peter also is an instance of Christ's readiness to forgive penitents. Peter was a member of that congregation in the midst of which Christ sung praises to His Father (Psalm 22:22). Peter fell foully, he denied his Master with oaths and curses, a horrid crime! Did Christ immediately cut him off? No, but admonished him by a look; the offender repented; the penitent was forgiven. Let churches follow the example which Christ has set them.

The act of excommunication may not be performed by a member on himself; such a one, said Dr. Gill, is a *felo de se*, he is, in effect, a self-murderer. As consent is necessary to a person's coming into the church, so none can go out of it without its consent. To attempt it is to break covenant with the church, and, as much as in a man lies, to break up the church. By the same rule that one member may thus leave the church, another may, the pastor may, all may; the tendency of which conduct, all may see is confusion and destruction. Those, therefore, who are guilty of it, ought to be looked upon as trucebreakers, proud, arrogant, dangerous persons, and to be dealt with as such. And they should be avoided by all other churches.

No man has a right of himself to perform this censure; it is a punishment inflicted by many (2 Corinthians 2:6). But this great censure is to be executed "by the elders [ministers] of churches, with the consent of the members of them; for they have a right to do this, previous to their having elders, and when they have none, as to receive members, so to expel them. The power of it originally lies in the church; the authority of executing it lies in the elders, with the consent and by the order of the church; as the directions to the churches concerning this matter, testify" (Gill).

To proceed regularly in this solemn business the church must cite an accused member to appear, either at a stated church meeting of business, or at an occasional meeting for that purpose; in order that he may have a fair trial and an opportunity of making his *defense* if he has any to make. The meeting is opened by prayer for direction; then the case is impartially examined and tried by the Word of God; if the accused member is found guilty of a crime deserving excommunication, he is not to be immediately cut off (unless it be some extraordinary case) but admonished, and some time given him for repentance and for the church to mourn over him and pray for him. If the offender continues obstinate and appears to be incorrigible, the church is under a necessity of proceeding to the execution of the great censure against him.

If the offense be private the censure may, and in some cases ought to be laid on before the church only; but if the crime is public, and very notorious, the honor of Christ calls for the censure to be public (1 Timothy 5:20, Jude 15). In this case the church appoints the day and summons the guilty member to attend; the minister suits his sermon to the occasion, after which he prays to God for a blessing on the ordinance to be administered; and then proceeds to sum up the sentence of the church; lays open the odious nature of the crime and the dreadful load of guilt which the sin, with its aggravations, has brought on the offender; he takes notice of the scandal it has brought on religion, how dishonorable to God, and grievous to the church; he observes that the excommunicating act is not intended for the destruction of the soul, but is used as a last remedy for the recovery of the offender, and as a caution to others. Then, by the authority of the Lord Jesus Christ, and in the name and behalf of that church, he cuts off and secludes the offender by name from union and communion with the church; he having broke his covenant with them, they also excluded him from the privileges of a member, as unworthy; yet praying the Lord Jesus Christ, who is the Good Shepherd, to restore him by giving him unfeigned repentance that he may again be received into the sheepfold.

If the accused member should obstinately refuse to appear before the church, when cited as above, it is to be deemed a sign of guilt, a contempt of the authority of the church, and an aggravation of his crime; and the process of the church against him, should not be obstructed on account of his absence.

If it should happen, that the minister of the church is the offender or that the church is without a minister, in either of these cases, they ought to call one from a sister church to assist them on such an occasion; for, as has been before observed, the authority of execution this censure (as well as all other ordinances in general) lies in the elders.

The ends to be answered by this solemn ordinance, and which should always be aimed at in the administration of it, are (1) the glory of God, which is the ultimate end of it, for as His name is dishonored by the evil practices or principles of church members, so this is the most open and most effectual way of removing the dishonor that is brought upon it; (2) another end is to purge the church and preserve it from infection, *a little leaven leavens the whole lump*, and therefore *the old leaven* must be purged out, that the church may become *a new lump; evil communications corrupt good manners*, and therefore evil men must be put away from among the saints (1 Corinthians 5:6, 7, 13). Lepers were to be put out of the camp that they might not infect others, and erroneous persons, whose words do eat as a canker, must be removed from the communion of churches; (3) a church of Christ is like a garden or vineyard, which, if not taken care of, as it is not, when this ordinance of excommunication is neglected, will be like the vineyard of the slothful, overrun with thorns, nettles, and other weeds; but by means of this it is cleared of the weeds of immorality, the bitter roots of false doctrines eradicated, and withered branches gathered and cast out; (4) and the good of persons excommunicated is another end which is sometimes effected by it, God blessing His own institution when rightly performed, which is for edification and not destruction; and for the saving of the souls of men who are hereby brought to shame and repentance for their sins, in which case they are to be received again with all love and tenderness and to be comforted that they may not be *swallowed up with overmuch sorrow* (Jude 23; 2 Thessalonians 3:14, 15; 2 Corinthians 2:7).

VI. Of the Association of Churches

AS the communion of saints, so the communion of churches is a desirable blessing. To obtain and promote which ought to be the study and endeavor of all the people of God.

Although churches formed on the gospel plan are independent of each other with regard to power, yet not so, strictly speaking, with regard to communion. For as saints in general have an indisputable right to share in each other's gifts and graces, so have churches in this joint capacity. It is a general rule, *to do good, and to communicate forget not* (Hebrews 13:16), which is applicable in a particular manner to churches as such.

In order the more amply to obtain this blessing of communion, there ought to be a coalescing or uniting of several churches into one body, so far as their local situation and other circumstances will admit. But as it is impracticable for all the individual members thus to associate and coalesce together, the churches should each respectively choose and delegate some of the most able, pious, and judicious from among themselves, and particularly their ministers, to convene at such times and places as may be thought most conducive to the great end proposed, and to act as their representatives in the general assembly. Their expenses ought to be defrayed by the churches who send them.

It appears advisable that these delegates, at their first meeting, should in a formal manner enter into covenant with each other, as the representatives of the churches, for the promoting of Christ's cause in general and for the interest of the churches they represent in particular. They should then form their plan of operation and fix on the most proper time and place for meeting in the future. Once a year at least they ought to meet at the place the most central and convenient for all the churches in confederation to attend.

Although such a conjunction of churches is not expressly commanded in Scripture, yet it receives sufficient countenance and authority from the light of nature and the general laws of society, but more especially from a precedent established by Apostolical authority (Acts 15).

The association thus formed is a respectable body as it represents not a city, country, or nation, but the churches of Jesus Christ. Yet it is by no means to be deemed a superior judicature vested with coercive power or authority over the churches; it presumes not to impose its sentiments on its constituents, under pain of excommunication; nor does it anathematize those who do not implicitly submit to its determinations, which would be nothing less than spiritual tyranny and better comport with the arbitrary spirit of popish councils than with that meekness which distinguishes the true disciples and humble followers of the lowly yet adorable Jesus. The apostles, elders, and brethren who composed the first Christian council presumed not to impose their conclusions on the churches in such a lordly manner, but prefaced their determinations with this modest prologue, *It seemed good to the Holy Ghost, and to us, to lay upon you no greater burden than these necessary things* (Acts 15:28). The Baptist Association therefore arrogates no higher title than that of an Advisory Council, consistent with which epithet, it ought ever to act, when it acts at all, without intruding on the rights of independent congregational churches or usurping authority over them (Matthew 23:10–12).

Nevertheless, the association has a natural and unalienable right to judge for itself what churches shall be admitted into confederacy with it, and to withdraw from all acts of communion and fellowship with any church, so admitted, provided such church should obstinately persist in holding corrupt principles, or indulging vicious practices, notwithstanding all proper endeavors have been used to reclaim it (Ephesians 5:7; Revelation 18:4).

It is generally agreed that an association when transacting business, should proceed in the following manner: (1) always begin and end each session by prayer; (2) admit none as messengers but such as come recommended by letters, well authenticated, from the churches to which they belong or from whence they come; (3) when a church petitions by letter for admission, if approved of, the moderator is to inform the messengers that their request is granted and desire them to take their seats; (4) all who have anything to offer are to rise and address the moderator; (5) while one is speaking, the rest are to be silent, yet all have an equal right to speak in turn; (6) no partiality or respect of persons is to be shown; (7) every matter should be canvassed with gravity, modesty, and a sincere aim to truth; (8) when all are not agreed, the matter may be put to the vote, and a majority determines; (9) all queries regularly sent by the churches should be answered, if possible; (10) any matter proposed, relative to the general good of the churches, should be seriously attended to; (11) every transaction should be conformable to the revealed will of God; (12) and a circular letter should be written and sent to all the churches in confederation containing such instruction, information, and advice as may be thought most suitable; and with which should be sent the transactions of the association.

The benefits arising from an association and communion of churches are many; in general, it will tend to maintain the truth, order, and discipline of the gospel. By it (1) the churches may have such doubts as arise among them cleared, which will prevent disputes (Acts 15:28, 29); (2) they will be furnished with salutary counsel (Proverbs 11:14); (3) those churches which have no ministers may obtain occasional supplies (Song of Solomon 8:8); (4) the churches will be more closely united in promoting the cause and interest of Christ; (5) a member who is aggrieved through partiality or any other wrongs received from the church may have an opportunity of applying for direction; (6) a godly and sound ministry will be encouraged, while a ministry that is unsound and ungodly will be discountenanced; (7) there will be a reciprocal communication of their gifts (Philippians 4:15); (8) ministers may alternately be sent out to preach the gospel to those who are destitute (Galatians 2:9); (9) a large party may draw off from the church by means of an intruding minister, or other ways, and the aggrieved may have no way of obtaining redress but from the association; (11) contentions may arise between sister churches, which the association is most likely to remove; (12) and the churches may have candidates for the ministry properly tried by the association.

These and other advantages arising from an association must induce every godly church to desire a union with such a body. But should any stand off, it would argue much self-sufficiency (Revelation 3:17), and little or no desire after the unity of the Spirit (Ephesians 4:3), or mutual edification (1 Corinthians 12:11–14).

THE END